Daddy is Dea

Introduction

This is a true story about a damaging father and son relationship and my recovery from addiction. I was born in Ireland in 1975, the youngest of nine children. My destructive father ripped through the heart of the family and his tyrannical nature has shaped many lives. All of my siblings hated him and got away from him as soon as they could. But I was developed to become his supporter and right-hand man. This role gave me a childish sense of power in our dysfunctional home. I stood by and witnessed his abuse, but deep down, I understood that he was a dark and dangerous man.

Inevitably, confusion and conflict drove me to run away

to England when I was nineteen years old. There were many new starts, bouncing from place to place, but his shadow followed me. Unresolved trauma created a brash ego and reckless man. I was unable to regulate my emotions or accept any form of love. Repetitive self-sabotage, compulsive behaviour and broken relationships consumed my adult life throughout my twenties. Mammy died as I started my thirties and I blocked the grief with cocaine. By the time I reached forty, all the signs indicated that it was not going to end well. But there is also a parallel narrative about the determination of a mother and how her eternal love protected me. At the edge of life, I was saved in the most extraordinary way. This experience became the spark that compelled me to write and face the truth.

17. New Life

1. Rock Bottom

My partner smiled and waved goodbye to me as she headed into the airport to catch her flight to Poland on a Tuesday morning in the summer of 2016. She was going to see her parents for a couple of weeks and this would leave me alone in our London flat with only my addiction for company. I promised her that I would behave, but that was a lie. Less than one hour later, I was in a pub and having my first drink. Next step was to get my hands on some strong cocaine via a reliable dealer. This was not a problem. About thirty minutes later, I made my first purchase of many in that week, buying five grams initially. Any thoughts of the hurt I was going to cause my partner and everyone who cared about me were shut away. I was forty-one years old at this stage and I had been running away and trying to escape from the truth for my entire life.

I was shaking with excitement as I parked my car outside our flat in leafy North London. The door key was pushed through the lock with laser focus and urgency, as I ran inside to get things started. I have often seen homeless addicts moving with the same anxious purpose when they are about to use drugs. They all unconsciously accelerate towards their next narcotic hit with tunnel vision. I might have believed that cocaine was cool or glamorous when I started taking it regularly in clubs and parties. But now, I was no different from those desperate homeless souls, possessed by addiction.

The table in the lounge was quickly cleared and I made a well-rehearsed start to proceedings;

Step 1: pour the lumpy, petrol-smelling cocaine out of the small plastic bags and onto a clean plate.

Step 2: chop and grind the lumps into a small mountain of fine crystallized powder with a credit card.

Step 3: roll a crisp new banknote and snort a huge intake up my nose to activate an instant and powerful dopamine hit.

The tension was building inside me for weeks, my nervous system was tingling and waiting to be medicated. I would always snort a full gram of stinging cocaine in that first initial intake. I wanted to get to oblivion as soon as possible. Starting my binge in such an extreme way caused me to fall down. I then just lay there and allowed the cocaine to overwhelm me, mouth drooling, nose running and slumped over on the floor. If anybody could see, they would have been disgusted and felt pity for me. This side of my addiction was best to be hidden away from judging eyes or anyone who would try to help me. There was also an added dimension and twist to my binges. Being able to access porn became inextricably linked to using cocaine. This combination was a very potent cocktail that I could not resist. A hotel room on a business trip or when my partner had to travel to Poland became opportunities and diary dates that shined like diamonds. Using cocaine in a social setting was long gone, replaced by something lonely, seedy and ugly.

After a couple of hours of cocaine mania that afternoon, I suddenly realised that I had to have a video call with my partner when she arrived in Poland. She would instantly know that I had relapsed if I missed the call. She had become an expert on my attempts to lie and cover up. I was going to counselling therapy for about a year at this stage, trying to stop my destructive habit. But each relapse then became an extreme binge and even more dangerous compared to how I used cocaine before. Just before the call, I took a cold shower to reduce the effects, but my face was still contorted and my speech was badly affected. It was a complete nightmare and I knew that my partner suspected something was wrong. I selfishly rushed the conversation so that I could get back to my cocaine and porn party for one. Later on, I sent a text message to confirm her suspicions were accurate. I then turned off my phone, locked the flat door with the double lock and I took the key inside under my control. Nothing was going to stop me pushing my life to the edge and destroying everything good along the way.

The initial supply of five grams lasted for a little over a day. I had to arrange for my drug dealer to deliver more to my flat on a few occasions through the week to keep the binge going at full speed. Time and reality became twisted, as I fell into the darkness. At one stage, I took the duvet cover from the bedroom and I was hiding under it on the sofa, like a naughty child hides from a parent when they have done something wrong. I wanted to escape myself and be invisible to the world. With so much stimulant in my system, sleep and food were not possible. I found myself pacing back and forth for hours and speaking to myself in a negative loop. I was worthless and I told myself that everyone would be better off without me. Shame and despair were finally going to swallow me up. This hell started on Tuesday and continued without a break through the week and into the weekend.

The cocaine supply ran out on Saturday and my drug dealer stopped answering my calls. He knew that it was risky visiting my flat and giving me more, considering my dangerous state. A taxi transported me to Soho after a quick clean up and fresh clothes. Some bars and a strip club were frequented, drinking, snorting and spending recklessly. As Saturday night drifted into Sunday morning, I got a taxi home with a small stash of cocaine in my pocket to last a few more hours. My final resting place was lying on the sofa on Sunday morning. About twenty grams of very strong cocaine had been consumed over the six days, plus plenty of alcohol on top. My nose was bleeding heavily and my eyes were streaming. I was not crying, I think that my nervous system was simply overloaded and sending confused signals. My muscles started to shake, my heart rate was accelerating and my chest was getting tighter and tighter. I knew that I had gone too far and I was unable to call for help. This was the end, I was alone, paralysed and terrified.

"Eternal Protection"

Despite being in such a defeated state and having no mechanical control over my body, something told me to breathe slowly and try to hold on. This sudden determination was not an accident, someone was watching over me. There was an energy just outside of my peripheral vision on the other side of the room. Mammy passed away nine years before, but I could feel her spirit with me and she was ready to help. I was so scared and numb that I spoke to her in a gentle whisper. I said: "Mammy, let me live and I promise I will stop". These words were repeated over and over, closing my eyes and focusing deeply on what it meant. My life was in her hands.

I had to concentrate on breathing, try not to panic and hope that my dangerous heart rate would eventually return to normal. The day passed by very slowly, as I struggled to ride it out and gradually step back from the edge. After a few hours, I tried to gently flex my hands and my feet as a first step, whilst still concentrating intently on breathing in a calm manner. There was light at the end of the tunnel, but I had to crawl there very carefully. I remained stuck in the same place on the sofa all day, it was not possible to move. My breathing was still very laboured as the evening approached, I was not able to stand up, but the worst of it had passed. Finally, late Sunday night, I managed to fall asleep on the sofa and bring the curtains down on this crisis. I was very lucky to survive. My addiction brought me to many dark places, but this specific binge was rock bottom. The most terrifying part was that I was unable to understand why I was trying to destroy myself or how I could stop. I can now see that I was repeatedly pushing myself into dangerous situations to shatter reality and confront my childhood trauma.

2. Daddy & Mammy

At the start of this catharsis, I was eager to document every traumatic and painful incident that happened in my family over the years. The negative consequences of enduring my father's abuse for all of us is very evident. I am the youngest of nine children and we seem so different on the surface. But now I can see that all of us feel the same shame and have become damaged adults in similar ways. Isolation, dysfunctional relationships, harmful coping mechanisms and mental illness have dominated our lives. The opposing influence of my parents is the most significant contribution to this story. I will also reveal a shocking family betrayal that has been hiding in plain view for decades, and not everyone will be happy about that. However, I will not describe what happened to each and every sibling. This is not my responsibility. But some characters in the family have an undeniable role in the narrative. There will be an appearance from a Robot, a Rattlesnake and a Rebel.

"Daddy"

My father was born in 1930 and grew up in rural County Limerick. He was the oldest child from a large family and he had to grow up fast when his father was absent or away working in England. Daddy left school early to support his mother as she struggled to bring up seven children. His mother was a fierce little woman, and she expected much from her son. Most of Ireland was trapped in abject poverty in that era. They lived in a humble terraced house. Hunting rabbits for food and finding firewood for warmth was a daily task. Daddy sometimes talked about helping his mother to wash clothes for people in the town willing to pay for the service. I sensed that this was a humiliating role and he held onto his resentment. This formative hardship stayed with him throughout his life, and the only women that he ever admired were aggressive and domineering types like his mother.

Daddy's mother died when I was a young boy and I can't remember meeting her. But I do have some very clear memories of my grandfather. I visited London when I was around seven years old with my father during the summer for a "holiday", but it was not very pleasant. We stayed with my auntie, a selfish and vicious woman, and my grandfather lived around the corner. Some tourist activities kept Daddy and me busy in the daytime, but he was going through the motions. The strongest memory I retained was him constantly pulling me by the ear and snarling if I walked off or asked a childish question. Going back to my auntie's house in the evening gave me a feeling of dread. I had to sit at the dinner table and try to digest some disgusting food, whilst she talked about herself and looked at me with daggers if I dared to make a face. I knew to keep my head down, otherwise, I would be on the receiving end of punishment before going to bed.

Visiting my grandfather was also gloomy. He was a physically imposing man in his prime, thick-set, handsome with piercing eyes. Even now, when I look into his face in old photos, I can somehow feel his primal nature staring back at me. Being in his presence as a child made me uneasy and timid. He was a dark and intense man. He lived on his own on the ground floor of a large apartment block and his flat was gloomy and cold. The only sound in his home was a sinister grandfather clock. The tick tock rhythm punctuated the tense atmosphere and let me know that I should not speak in his presence. There was no space there for warmth, play or joy.

Towards the end of the holiday, I was very sick with a stomach bug. Vomiting and diarrhoea were a serious inconvenience for my father and auntie. They looked at me with disgust and left me alone with my grandfather whilst they went out for the day. It was a very long day and I can't remember him checking on me. I can only remember being isolated in a cold room and suffering through the fever. My vicious auntie informed me that the cause of my stomach upset was an insect having a shit on my food. A horrible piece of information that did nothing to aid my recovery. I then felt guilty for not noticing the insect and causing such a nuisance for others. That miserable trip to London was my only holiday as a child.

A couple of years later, I was brought to London as my father's travel companion when my grandfather was in hospital following a gruesome leg amputation. He died shortly after and I was brought back to London again to assist at the funeral. Even though I was very young, I can clearly remember that it was a strange event, Daddy did not cry and he never mentioned his father again. Only now have I started to look into the past and piece together the hushed-up stories hiding under the surface. I was told that my grandfather was a serial womaniser with no boundaries in his younger days and that he fathered a child with his wife's sister. He then forced his fierce wife to bring up the illegitimate child with her own biological children. This unfortunate child was abused because of what she represented. My father witnessed this dysfunction whilst growing up and it shaped him.

Daddy inherited many of his father's physical characteristics. He was stocky, with thick limbs and cold blue eyes that could look right through you. Heavily tattooed arms and hands were part of his intimidating body language. If you were unlucky enough to hold eye contact with him for more than a few seconds, you would see his gold tooth within his signature nasty smile. When I was five years old, my father was fifty, but he seemed to have the strength of a much younger man. Lifting the limbs of oak trees was made to look easy, like they were made of paper. Added to his physical powers, Daddy had an intense presence, which gave him the ability to unnerve people and control a room when he wanted to. He was a highly perceptive man who could quickly work people out, assign value to them and plan how he intended to use people for his own benefit.

"Mammy"

My mother was born in 1931, also in rural County Limerick and somewhere in the middle of a large family. Her home was a humble stone cottage set on the side of a hill, surrounded by lush green fields and overlooked by a pine wood. This little postcard image house was a picturesque and peaceful place to grow up. Mammy was a pretty young girl, a petite brunette with a warm smile and kind eyes. A sweet-natured and trusting person, always seeing the better parts of people and overlooking character flaws. Mammy was never academic or ambitious and she left school in her early teens to find work with a basic education. I have limited knowledge of Mammy's parents, they both died many years before I was born. I don't know anything significant about her mother, I sense that she was closer to her father. From what I know, her father was a good man but he had poor physical health. He suffered a brain tumour and died when Mammy was still a teenager. It must have been a real struggle for the family left behind. Mammy had brothers, but they were not strong men, and they would not be able to protect her from a predator.

Mammy often talked about going to the dance in the town hall on a Saturday night when she was a teenage girl. She loved getting dressed up and dancing, and she attracted the attention of many. Her admirers lined up and paraded themselves in their second-hand suits, offered to buy her cigarettes and walk her home, hoping that they would be picked. Mammy met my father when she was just fifteen years old and she immediately fell for his brutal charm. She often talked about how he romanced her and how he was violent towards other men if they looked in her direction. Perhaps his territorial aggression was mistaken for romantic jealously in the early stages of their relationship.

One night she allowed another young man to walk her home from the town after a dance. The roads were very isolated and dark and she was a teenage girl, the act was friendly and innocent. She did not realise that Daddy was watching from a distance and silently following behind. Daddy concealed himself behind a wall and jumped out to launch a surprise attack. The unlucky young man was punched and kicked to the ground. When Daddy had delivered a sufficient beating, he picked up the young man's bicycle and threw it at his grounded opponent to make sure that the message was understood. Mammy did not enjoy violence, it was not in her nature.

But she was too young to fully grasp the kind of man she was destined to spend her life with.

"Secret Baby"

My parents went to England in their teenage years to work. Mammy headed for London to become a housemaid, but I was told that Daddy moved around England and worked in many different places. To travel from rural Ireland to London in the late 1940s was a huge leap for a teenage girl. However, "going to England" also served another unspoken purpose back then and for many decades after. Countless working-class Irish families were forced to cover up at least one birth that was out of wedlock in some desperate way. There are too many tragic stories of secret babies hidden and given away to preserve so-called Christian dignity. It’s strange to think that the bond between a mother and child could be the source of lies and secret arrangements. Mammy was pregnant and she made the journey to London to hide her baby from the damnation of backward Ireland. She was vulnerable and far away from home, but Daddy kept his distance to protect his reputation and avoid his responsibility.

Mammy worked as a maid for a Jewish family and she lived with her wealthy employers in their north London mansion. The head of the family was a gentleman, who loved to share a joke and a laugh with Mammy. She told me that he called her “little Annie” and maybe his caring nature helped her to cope with the loss of her own father. Whilst living with the Jewish family, she gave birth to a baby boy. However, her first precious child died when he was just two months old, or so the story was told many years later. Who knows what happened, there are so many questions that may never be answered. Where was my father at that time of the birth? What sickness killed the baby? Where was the little body buried? How is his life marked in this world? Mammy carried this secret and pain throughout her life.

Despite the devastating loss, Mammy somehow got back on her feet with help from her Jewish employer. She continued with London life and she met a new boyfriend. I don't know that much about this man, I am searching my memory as I write this story to recall what Mammy told me when I was a very small child. I believe he was English and he treated Mammy very well from the fragments that I can recall. Her voice sounded happy when she talked about this time of independence from my father. It's hard to think about my mother choosing a different life long before I was born, a life that would cancel my existence. But it was a short romance and my father made his move to take her back. Now that the baby was gone and the risk of social shame had passed over, he decided to seize his property.

Daddy wrote romantic letters, he knew how to manipulate a young woman who still loved him deep down. He was very persistent and driven to get what he wanted. The Jewish family begged Mammy to stay with them in London, they loved her like a daughter and they wanted the best for her. They had witnessed her suffering and maybe they sensed that a life with Daddy would not be a good life. But their efforts to keep Mammy in London were in vain. Daddy took her back to rural County Limerick, a place where he had all of the advantages to control her. Allowing Mammy to have any form of freedom was a threat and he would not make that mistake again.

My parents got married around 1950 and started a family. Daddy joined the army and they moved into a little army terraced house in the Curragh. The army provided opportunities for my father. He became a radio technician and he was promoted very quickly. His smart uniform and shiny badges gave him the mask that he needed to distract people from his underlying nature. The army also brought my father to many places in the world whilst serving with the United Nations. However,

Mammy was left with no money to take care of their young children when he was away. He benefited from his regular military salary and an additional payment for his overseas duties, but this money was for him. Daddy somehow made her believe that he received no salary whilst he was away. Mammy was forced to give her children to one of her brothers to look after, whilst she went to work in a factory in England to make money. Her compliance and acceptance of his lies informed my father that he could push the boundaries in this marriage even further.

3. Strange Home

My parents lived on the army base for many years, a place where Mammy felt relatively safe. She was a social creature and she could easily access friends living in a tight community of terraced houses. Daddy did not like this and he wanted to find a property with more privacy. He had saved enough money to purchase a house with cash, an unusual and suspicious achievement for a man employed by the army. My family moved into their new home in a small village located about a mile from the military base in the late 1960s. The house was a detached cottage, with a very large garden and plenty of uninhabited land surrounding the house on each side and at the rear. There were no close neighbours, only the front of the house was visible to passers-by on the road. A space where Daddy's behaviour could be concealed.

Mammy told me that her new neighbours would shake her hand as they met on the road and comment on how pretty and respectable her new home was. The garden was surrounded by well-groomed hedges and filled with flowers and trees bearing fruit. My father cut down the trees and set about creating the miserable and ugly home that he desired. The cottage was not modern and needed regular maintenance, but it was deliberately allowed to deteriorate. Daddy started many large and ambitious projects but abandoned the work very quickly, forcing everyone to live in the chaos he created.

By the time I arrived in 1975, the house was on the very edge of functioning, patched together with rusty nails and pieces of old wood. Broken walls, leaking pipes, exposed electrical wires and holes in the floor were the norm. There were deep trenches in the kitchen floor that went right down to our damp foundations and exposed the muddy soil under the house. After a cold winter night, we were greeted with glimmering snail trails on the kitchen wall in the morning, as the snails moved up from the frosty earth to find warmth. Daddy used to laugh and celebrate the shiny patterns weaving all over the kitchen, knowing that it repulsed us. I can remember a sustained period in my childhood when there was no working bathroom, central heating or floorboards in half of the house. We used an assault course of narrow makeshift planks to travel from room to room. One of my nephews fell through the hole in the floor and was hospitalised, lucky not to have permanent damage, but the floor was left as it was.

"Public Image"

Our home was chaotic and miserable on the inside, but Daddy was careful about maintaining his external image and public veneer. The front of our house was painted, flowers planted and the grass was cut in a few selected places where it could be seen from the road. At a glance, strangers walking or driving past were unaware of the destruction going on behind the scenes. Daddy also managed his public outings effectively, he drove a good car and wore expensive clothes. He knew how to turn on a fake smile and charm when encountering people that he wanted to impress. But once he was at home, the clean-cut act was immediately ditched for soiled clothes and a scowling face that told you, "Do not approach me".

We also had to endure Daddy's filthy and weird personal hygiene. He always left the toilet door open whilst defecating. The toilet was next to our kitchen, he wanted you to hear and smell him marking his territory. He delighted in displaying his broken and dirty toenails whilst sitting at the kitchen table. His next trick was to instruct one of our dogs to lick his mouldy feet until they were clean. There were also other behaviours that I now realise were beyond strange. Daddy urinated in plastic bottles during the night and stored them in the bedroom that he shared with Mammy. Every morning, his bottled yellow piss was deployed as fertilizer for the tomatoes and vegetables in the garden. Daddy was feeding us his filth.

Mammy was tasked with preparing and serving three solid meals every day for my father. Breakfast was muesli and grapefruit, a salad for lunch and his dinner was always potatoes, vegetables and some form of meat. This system was delivered consistently, almost like a ritual. Daddy looked after his diet, growing organic food for himself in the garden, he understood the science of food and how it can support good health. When he arrived home for lunch or after work, we instinctively knew to leave the kitchen area. The noise of the gate opening and his car pulling in was an alarm for everyone to get to their feet and get out of his way. The kitchen table was very small with just two accessible places,

"Daddy's chair" and another chair that nobody dared to use. This was a deliberate anti-family design.

I can count on one hand the number of times I have seen Mammy sitting down to eat. She seemed to survive on cups of tea and secret cigarettes. She had to sneak each cigarette behind my father's back or whilst he was at work. He knew that she smoked, he used to buy her cigarettes when they were teenagers to charm her. But once they were married he decided that cigarettes were banned. Mammy was constantly penniless, but she managed to access cigarettes here and there from other smokers to keep her going. It was not her health that he was concerned with, it was the cost of the cigarettes and the pleasure they gave her that he wanted to control.

"Running Away"

I have a very vivid memory of wandering away from home when I was around three years old. It is one of my first and most powerful memories. Mammy must have been busy and whilst she was temporarily distracted, I managed to navigate my way through a gap in the wall and walk a long way into a large field that lay behind our house. We had a big black and white sheepdog at that time, I remember that he came with me for some reason. He was watching over me like a wise sentinel, patiently guarding me on my journey. I found a large fallen tree on the far side of the field and started to play on it. This old tree became my new fantasy home, I was chatting away, a little man and a big dog striking out in this new world together. I was so far away that I would have been invisible to anyone looking for me. If I cried or called out, nobody would have been able to hear me or see me. There were cattle and horses in those fields, a few steps in the wrong direction and I could have been seriously hurt or much worse.

I can only imagine the emotions that erupted in Mammy when she realised that she could not find me, an instant and overwhelming desperation. Mammy must have searched our house and garden first, it was the obvious place to look. She then began to search the fields behind the house, maybe I had tried to go out there before. She eventually saw me in the distance and I can remember her calling my name with the purest relief in her voice as she approached. Even now, I can close my eyes and see Mammy running towards me with her apron still on and a tea towel clenched tightly in her right hand. She was baking when she realised I was not there and she was so tense during the frantic search, that she forgot to let go of the tea towel. She ran towards me with short rapid steps and then embraced me with pure love. I believe that this childish exploration was the start of my instinct to run away from home.

Mammy's existence meant that our home was not always harsh and tense. By contrast, when Daddy was at work the place was like another world for a little while. If we knew that he was away for several hours, we could relax and behave differently without being self-conscious. I can remember being alone with Mammy many times as a small child. The radio would be on and Mammy would be singing and skipping across the kitchen, chatting casually and giving me smiles, eye contact and soft touches. The smell of freshly baked bread and apple tarts added even more comfort to these moments. The atmosphere had a real warmth and tenderness. Even though I was small, I could somehow sense that it was ok for Mammy to give me all of her attention. This could not happen if Daddy was at home, his needs came before everyone else. The music would be switched off and any form of play or joy would not be tolerated in his presence.

"Name Calling"

I don't like being around shouting and aggressive name-calling. No matter what the situation is, any loud and high-pitched argument makes me uncomfortable and agitated. This goes back to my earliest childhood memories at home, silent tension progressively building, waiting for Daddy to select a target and a weak point. His name-calling and verbal assaults were like a hammer, constantly chipping away at your self-belief. Breaking your spirit was his favourite hobby and he looked visibly energised when he was mocking others. Mammy would ignore his attacks for hours, but eventually, she would be forced to respond and defend herself. Then came full aggression from Daddy, shouting at Mammy, escalating and escalating, louder and louder.

Daddy had a selection of attacks, angles and traps to degrade us. If Mammy didn't do something around the house correctly he called her "bird brain", letting her know that she was stupid and worthless. It could be the most trivial thing, not knowing how to switch on the radio or find a programme on the TV. This was an opportunity to pound her for hours with "I am the only intelligent person in this house" and "manufacturer's instructions are a waste of time for stupid people". If anyone left a light switched on for a second longer than necessary, we would be informed about who was paying the bills and that we contributed nothing. The perverse thing was that Daddy rigged the meter and the electricity was virtually free. But he still found a way of making us feel that we owed him something. We all knew that the meter was rigged, but we did not dare bring that up when he attacked. Better to just take his abuse and keep your head down.

Another persistent and reliable attack was calling Mammy a "drug addict" for having a secret smoke. This usually came when the fridge was empty, which was often, or if she asked for anything for her children. We were deprived by him, but he managed to twist the story into Mammy being a bad mother and dependent on him to survive. He never asked us if we had eaten or had any consideration for what we had eaten. His diet was well-balanced and nutritious, but our diet and eating habits developed badly. Opening the fridge was not acceptable in his presence, so we rushed any food consumption if we knew that he was due home. I have only recently noticed that I frequently eat standing up or walking, because taking a seat at his table was risky. I have also developed a love for eating take away food in isolation. A bag of chips and a cheeseburger on the go has always been a source of comfort, replacing the space where there should have been a relaxed and nourishing family meal.

Once he started on you, it was a no-win situation. If he couldn't get a reaction from Mammy, he then started on her children. This was guaranteed to make her bite back and allowed him to dish out the insults that were already carefully prepared hours earlier. Daddy blamed Mammy for anything negative that happened to her children. Historical or current issues were brought up and dragged through the mud repetitively. Not finishing school, broken relationships, unemployment, substance abuse, he was not fussy. All of it was pushed in her direction, but the truth is that he caused these developmental and behavioural problems. Things were simplified to nasty categories for his own children, "wasters" for the boys and "bitches" for the girls.

I can remember listening to Mammy and Daddy arguing one night in the kitchen. I must have been very small because I was looking up at them. The shouting was relentless, Mammy was fighting back and the argument seemed to be going on and on for hours. Eventually, I decided I was going to show them how to be good parents. I was crying, but I built myself up and I suddenly intervened to stop proceedings. I said: "Why are we always shouting at each other?" and for a moment they were both shocked at my unexpected outburst. There was a very temporary silence, and then Daddy blamed Mammy, saying that she was responsible for upsetting a child and he walked out of the room with his victory. Then back to silent tension again, waiting anxiously for his next attack.

“School Party”

Any form of celebration at home were generally banned by Daddy, unless he had something to gain from it. But there were parties at school from time to time. I have a clear memory of a party at school when I was around six years old. On a pre-planned day, every child was expected to bring in sweets, cakes and fizzy drinks to share with the class. I brought sandwiches of lettuce from our garden and I was embarrassed when the other kids asked me why I did not have any sweets. I told them that I loved lettuce that was grown in our garden and it was my favourite food in the world. The other kids and the teacher felt sorry for me, but I did not accept their offer to share with me. I knew that if I accepted their sweets, I would give the game away. This was the start of being prepared to deny my father's tyranny at all costs. Mammy knew that I would be embarrassed and it must have broken her heart that day. No doubt that she asked Daddy for some money the day before, and he enjoyed saying no.

"Bed Wetting"

I frequently woke up in the morning to a wet bed as a child. I can remember feeling ashamed, but at times, I can also remember being conscious that I was wetting myself and allowing it to happen. I secretly hoped that my badly timed excretions would get the attention of my dysfunctional parents. Mammy was always the one dealing with the wet sheets, whilst scampering nervously around the house tending to Daddy and helping her children prepare for school. My bedwetting was a disruptive incident for Mammy and she always tried her best to cover it up. However, this became more and more challenging, I was wetting the bed so often and we were obviously not stocked up with fresh sheets. Each incident had to be hidden from Daddy to make sure a bad situation was not made worse.

One morning, Mammy found me stuck to the wet bedsheets once again and she started to cry. This was unusual, she rarely showed vulnerability, but she could not take any more pressure. I had to strip and stand naked in the front room to avoid Daddy who was eating in the kitchen. I stood there shivering and crying, whilst Mammy opened every drawer and cupboard to find something for me to use as underwear, but she could not locate anything useful. In desperation, she eventually gave me some of Daddy's oversized underwear to get me through the day. I put on my father's underwear reluctantly, folding and tucking the excessive and over-hanging material into my boyish trousers as best as possible. School was nerve-racking that day. I was hyper conscious that I was concealing my father's underwear and I was praying that there would not be a situation that would reveal my unfortunate position.

"Daddy's Helper"

The majority of my childhood motivations were focused on pleasing Daddy. Serving him ruled me. The more spirited and vocal members of the family were cast aside and ignored. They were categorised as "useless" and “troublemakers” because they could see him for what he was, and hence, they were invisible to him. I remember feeling that he wanted to turn me against the rest of the family. He was successful back then, but somewhere deep down, I was confused by the division. Daddy was always scheming and plotting and he gave me an obvious preference to develop my loyalty. Any minor conflict at home was developed into “them and us”, with me as his ally, standing behind him, attracted to the power that he held over everybody. When we were alone together he would say to me, “Don’t listen to them Patrick, you stick with me”. This gave me a false sense of security and I didn’t see or understand that that I was being pulled into his shadow.

Daddy was obsessed with hoarding firewood and coal for the range cooker we had at home. The coal was a premium fuel source and intended solely for warming the master of the house. This was stored in specific sheds and locks and barbed wire were used to protect the bags of coal that he counted on a regular basis. But whilst Daddy was out, Mammy would ask me to crawl through a small gap in the shed wall to steal a few lumps to keep the fire going during winter. I did help Mammy, but part of me knew I was being disloyal to Daddy. Old buildings and rubbish dumps were an opportunity to obtain free firewood and I was often left there with an empty trailer to fill whilst Daddy was at work. I was also expected to go out to the fields at night with Daddy to cut down trees to satisfy his obsession. This was not allowed by the farmers, so he chose the darkest winter nights with wet and windy weather to avoid detection. He was careful to cover the sawdust and any visible signs of the fresh cuts on the trees with mud.

Stealing wood from the fields was my chance to impress Daddy and I always attempted to carry more than I could manage. Struggling home under the weight of heavy branches and dragging them into our yard was an honour. The next task was to cut up the fresh wood into smaller pieces to cover the evidence. Daddy had a chainsaw, but that was too noisy and would draw attention late at night. I partnered with Daddy on the manual Two-Man-Saw, operated by two people, standing opposite each other, pushing and pulling in a timed rhythm together. We quickly sliced the trees into short blocks of wood that could be hidden in one of our sheds.

Daddy was aggressive with the Two-Man-Saw, pushing and pulling with force. I did my best to keep up with him, I wanted badly to show him that I had a strong right arm. Sometimes the saw jumped out of the cut because he was pulling it so hard, and I would let go of the handle. His look of disapproval was enough to make me feel weak. But I never gave up or refused to refuse to help him.

When Daddy and I were alone together in a shop, he would drag me close and whisper instructions to look straight ahead. He would then slip small items into my pockets to avoid paying. I knew that he was stealing and it made me nervous, but it was important to get his approval. Driving through the countryside was also an opportunity to steal. He would spot something valuable, maybe a bike, tools or metal. I was instructed to jump a wall or climb a fence to retrieve the desired object and I always completed the task efficiently. Daddy knew that I was driven to please him and he could blame me as a child if someone caught us, avoiding any embarrassment or legal implications for himself.

My admiration for my father grew and grew as I developed. I stared at his wallet when he pulled it out of his back pocket in shops, it was always packed with cash. Daddy often took me to the tailor's in the town to stand by and watch whilst he selected yet another new jacket that he would never wear. He had an impressive wardrobe filled with new clothes hanging in their plastic covers. Sometimes I would sneak into his bedroom whilst he was at work and discreetly inspect his wardrobe to marvel at his sartorial wealth. I can still visualise the rails loaded with expensive jackets, leather, tweed, suede, wool, mixed seasonal colours and styles, and always the best brands.

Daddy had an enviable wardrobe, whilst we had to live with second-hand clothes acquired from markets. Mammy would wait until the end of the day for the gipsies to throw away what they could not sell, and then pounce and fill plastic bags with the rejected items. I can still see Mammy dragging those bags of clothes home on her own, whilst neighbours watched through windows, sneered and whispered their judgments. When I was old enough, I used to help Mammy to carry the bags and we would go through the loot together. An Adidas tracksuit without any holes or maybe a wearable pair of jeans was an occasional bonus, but most of it was close to being rags.

Going back to school every September was an annual drama. A new uniform and books were required and every child had to comply. I was repeatedly embarrassed when the teachers asked why I did not have the correct uniform and I had to ask other children to share their books with me. Eventually, following a week of persistent begging, Daddy would slowly drip-feed some money to Mammy, but it was never quite enough. He was hoping that I would come by the necessary resources in another way. He enjoyed the begging and the stress it caused Mammy trying to find a way out of a corner.

However, if clothes were required for a public event that he was attending, he was careful to ensure that he was not embarrassed. As my Holy Communion approached when I was eight years, Mammy was very anxious, trying to pull together the right clothes to make sure I did not stick out. All the boys in my class got a new suit, new shoes and all the appropriate accessories for the occasion. Mammy managed to secure some second-hand black shoes and grey trousers for me, and she pushed Daddy to help with the rest as the date got uncomfortably close. I felt on top of the world when Daddy brought me to a shop and purchased a new navy blazer and blue shirt to complete my outfit. This would ensure that I was just about acceptable to stand next to him in the church grounds on the day. I can't remember any other occasion when my father bought clothes for me.

"Cruel Master"

The Cold War between the Soviet Union and America and the threat of nuclear destruction dominated the news through the 1980s. Daddy always admired dictators and there was a sparkle in his eye when he watched movies or documentaries about their evil deeds. He used to say "Hitler had the right idea" when he was promoting his bigoted and racist views. He also was interested in the history of the Soviet Union and he openly admired Stalin's murderous totalitarian system. I picked my father's side in the war that played out at home and his ideology became mine. My strange fascination with Soviet power extended to writing letters to the Soviet embassy in Ireland to request information. I created a school project honouring the "greatest nation on earth" and called myself "Comrade". My dedication and desire to embody what my father wanted went much further than normal. I wore military clothes, a balaclava at times and I carried a very large dagger. This behaviour was unhealthy for a child but it was useful to my father. He knew that I was ready to serve him and protect him.

We had several dogs at home and Daddy picked his "favourite" dog, an aggressive Jack Russell terrier called Lady. She was smaller than the other dogs, but she was able to dominate them with her fiery nature and my father's support. Maybe her character reminded him of his fierce mother. Occasionally some of our dogs would have unwanted puppies. This inconvenience was dealt with coldly. Daddy would simply snatch the poor whimpering souls from their mother and smash their tiny heads against a wall to end their short lives. Even more concerningly, an electric fence was erected on the flowers at the front of the house to keep the dogs off. The danger to children is obvious. The electric fence inevitably killed one of our dogs and I can remember finding his stiff and lifeless body amongst the flowers. He had got trapped on the wire whilst trying to escape the electric shock designed to deter him. I ran inside to inform Daddy, I was upset by the situation, but I knew that I could not show any emotion. Daddy picked up the dead body and disposed of it without a word to me. The electric fence stayed, as if nothing had happened.

"Money Power"

My father had a predatory eye for attractive women, he flirted and made crude advances whilst I was with him, especially when he was in his car. I was often in the passenger seat as he slowed down and pulled up close to his target, looking them up and down. Like a wolf isolating and stunning an unfortunate animal in its tracks with his cold blue eyes and sleazy charm. He had no shame and took advantage of any situation where women had no quick escape from him. Women working at the supermarket checkout or stuck at a service position in the bank were his favourite type of prey. Daddy would just stand there being suggestive, making them blush and look away, knowing that they could not easily escape him. The more embarrassed and bashful they were, the more he was energised. He flashed his wallet bulging with cash to demonstrate his status and get their attention.

Some of these women were uncomfortable, but some were fascinated and almost hypnotised by his crude confidence.

Daddy had multiple bank accounts and I was often his companion on trips to the banks in town. He would repeatedly draw out thousands of pounds from one bank, then walk across the road with the cash concealed inside his jacket, and deposit it in a different bank. A week later, he would reverse the transaction in the same way. I think he liked seeing the money and the sense of power it gave him in the bank. His financial resources forced the pretty girls to run around and work hard to please him. However, this wealth was concealed from our family and it was a resource that he never shared. If we asked him for a penny, he would say "Where would I get money from?". If Mammy said that she knew he had money, he would accuse her of being a spy and a thief. My position on the inside of Daddy's world made me feel like I held privileged information and even a certain level of authority in our home.

Mammy had to fight for her "housekeeping" money every week on a Thursday when Daddy came back from work. This measured money was used to purchase food to feed my father only and meet his exact dietary requirements. Our basic needs as children for food, clothes and schoolbooks were denied. We had to survive on a diet of chips made from potatoes from the garden and sugary homemade tarts from the apples gathered in my brother's orchard. If Mammy had a sneaky few pounds from somewhere under the radar, I was always the first to benefit. A green old Irish pound note in my pocket for lunch money, I was walking on air. I used to binge on sweets, spending it all in one go. Money became highly emotional for me, a dirty secret and something that I had to spend very fast.

There were three little local shops operating in our village. Groceries could be obtained on the "weekly bill", paying back at the end of the week or when you could afford. I remember that Mammy had a weekly bill in all three shops and she was not able to pay any of her debts. Sometimes she would send me in to get something on the weekly bill, hoping that I would be able to use my boyish charm to avoid payment requests. I didn't know what was going on, secrets, embarrassment and covering up. Mammy always used any spare cash she had to please others, never thinking of her own security and the longer term. This state of constant privation impacting her children must have hurt Mammy more than I can imagine.

"Workshop Theft 1"

Daddy kept bulky rolls of cash notes in his personal and sacred space, the workshop. This was a small room at the back of the house that was under lock and key. A place that was out of bounds for most of the family. However, I had a higher level of access, as his little helper. When Daddy was preparing for work, I was often sent to the workshops to get specific tools. He kept many secrets there, locked metal boxes holding official documents and stacks of cash under heavy objects to flatten the notes. Many times, when I moved tools around, I would accidentally discover a stack of £20 notes as thick as a book. We were so desperate and it was so tempting, I eventually took a single £20 note. It was the old Irish currency, the £20 note was a sky-blue colour, it was staring at me, telling me to take it. There was so much money, I hoped that Daddy would not miss it.

I was around ten years old when I did this for the first time and I gave the money directly to Mammy to help relieve her financial constriction. We then became an organised team and my workshop theft from Daddy became a regular event. Mammy would make a distraction in the kitchen, pouring tea or serving food and I would slip inside the workshop if the door was unlocked like a ninja, to lighten his stacks of cash by a crisp £20 note. I never took more than £20 in one go, but the overall amount was now building up. Sometimes I knew I was pushing my luck whilst he was still in the house, but I wanted to help Mammy and I continued to take the risk. It was only a matter of time before this would catch up with me. Sooner or later, he would count his money and my crime would be detected.

Mammy went out to see her friend every evening, at about 8 pm, coming home just before midnight. She walked down the road every night without fail, regardless of the weather conditions. This was her only chance to have a smoke and relax. She was also motivated by the free cigarettes her friend provided, which helped her to protect her own humble supply. Daddy didn't care about her social activity, just as long as Mammy did not ask him for any money and his meals were served. One night, whilst Mammy was out, I was asleep in bed when I was suddenly woken up by Daddy. He ordered to come out to the kitchen immediately, he was very angry and he had a wooden stick in his hand. I knew that it was going to be bad.

I stumbled dazed and confused into the bright lights of the kitchen, rubbing my eyes and shivering in my bare skin without pyjamas. Daddy was boiling with anger, he informed me that he knew that I had stolen cash from him and I was told to confess or face the consequences. He had waited until Mammy was out, knowing that she would try to save me from harm. He told me that if I confessed to the theft, he would not hurt me, waving the stick in my face. I fell into his trap and confirmed that I had done it. Now he had the evidence he needed and the green light to punish me. Despite his promise not to hurt me, Daddy hit me with the stick repeatedly until the stick broke on my body. I accepted my punishment, as usual, standing still and absorbing the blows.

After Daddy broke the stick, he then ordered me to wait in the kitchen and he went into his workshop. I stood there, trying to hold back the tears, terrified and wondering what was going to happen next. He returned quickly with a bigger stick, a much stronger weapon that would not fail or break. He delivered some further physical punishment with his more reliable weapon and my cries of "Sorry Daddy" did not stop him. When he was satisfied that he had administered sufficient punishment, he ordered me back to bed and he followed me to deliver a psychological blow to finish the job. He told me that I was a “disgusting thief” and that I “did not deserve to be under his roof”. That workshop theft was a major setback to my ambition to be his favourite. I now wanted to work even harder to be back on Daddy’s good side, and he was ruthless enough to allow me to ashamed of my crime.

“Workshop Theft 2”

The punishment that I received for the first theft was enough to deter me from that temptation for a few years. However, as time passed, I started to want the things that all young boys wanted, new trainers, football boots, branded tracksuits. I started to slip into Daddy’s workshops undetected once again to relieve him of a couple of £20 notes each time. The deal with Mammy was simple, one for her and one for me. This time we were equal partners and sharing the spoils of our crime. Daddy counted his money at regular intervals, so my day of reckoning was inevitable. This time he caught me in the act. He saw me walking out of his workshop suspiciously, he went inside and quickly established that there was cash missing. Mammy was also at home and she was terrified of the violent consequences. I stood still in the hallway, waiting for a punch in the face to get things started, but the physical blow did not come, much to my surprise.

Daddy decided to deploy a different strategy to punish me this time. I was a little older and maybe a wooden stick would be ineffective, or maybe I would fight back. A more long-lasting punishment was used to injure me for disloyalty. Daddy suddenly changed his mood and body language. He started to question me about how long it was going on and why I decided to betray him. I tried to explain that I needed things and that I was scared to ask for the money. Mammy joined me, we were standing together, heads down, a pair of convicts, guilty as charged. He saw an opportunity to nail both of us to the wall. Mammy was accused of corrupting a child and he looked at me with disgust and said “I thought you were different, but you are just like the rest”. This hurt me more than a physical blow and he walked off grinning, knowing that I would crawl back to him.

“American Show”

The dysfunction in our family was never more evident than when we had a visit from Daddy's sister from America. She had migrated to America as a young woman and she came back to Ireland with her grown-up children on a few occasions. Daddy did not want her to visit, we were an embarrassment to him, but if happened, a great show was put on. Suddenly the house had to be cleaned up and the chaos hastily disguised. Cheap wallpaper covered cracks and holes in the wall and damaged floors were concealed with temporary rugs. We were told with a stern voice and direct eye contact, "Shut up and don't talk until I tell you that you can talk". Expensive food was purchased and matching plates and cutlery were borrowed to support the illusion. Mammy and the less favoured children became the help, shuffling around in the background tending to the guests needs.

When the Americans arrived the energy in the house changed. We were all suddenly smiling pleasantly, nervous that our cover-up would be spotted. I knew that I had a duty in this tense situation, to impress and distract and I was wheeled out to amuse the visitors. I was talkative and very willing to be "Daddy's favourite", performing the act of a loving son. This was a prize for me, a badge to be worn with pride. I would get in the middle of the visitors and up close to Daddy, which helped him to appear as a normal father. This fraud hurt my siblings and impacted our future relationships.

During one particular visit, the Americans and our family went to the local pub. Alcohol flowed and this probably eased the tension and made the situation more bearable. After the pub closed, the party continued at my brother's house, a weird family "lock-in" with our American observers. My brothers and the husbands of my sisters were laughing together as men, they were feeling more confident around Daddy. With the Americans there, knowing that Daddy would not ruin his appearance, one of my sister's husbands used the opportunity to make a joke about Daddy in front of everyone. I was sitting next to Daddy and our relationship was jeered at. I was labelled his little disciple and we only had each other. Everybody laughed loudly in their temporary moment of freedom, but I didn't really understand the uncomfortable joke.

4. The Rattlesnake

I am going to confront a grotesque episode in my family history. It is the elephant in the room and a forbidden subject, because nobody knows exactly how to deal with it. Many family arguments and fights over the years were loaded with the weight of this betrayal, but it was never fully exposed. Around the time I was born, my father and a reptile accomplice took part in a brazen affair that defies belief. The stress and pain that Mammy endured during this time must have transferred into me as an infant. The long-term developmental consequences caused by being brought up in such a toxic environment are now very obvious. The lies and intimidation used to keep this affair from being discussed is at the core of our family dysfunction.

"The Robot"

One of my brothers is a compact and functional man on the surface. The Robot was studious in his youth and became a professional adult. But his mechanical movements, monotone voice and battery-operated personality did not command respect from his siblings. He took no genuine interest in our lives and I can't remember any occasion where he had a real conversation with me. Pursuing crafts was more important than making friends and being social. One of his hobbies was making ships in bottles, which is a suitable metaphor for his own life. A small and pointless object confined and controlled in an ornamental world. The most significant thing that ever happened to him was his unfortunate choice of spouse. The Robot married a narcissistic woman and this foolish act had far reaching consequences. She programmed him to follow her instructions and he allowed an unbelievable intrusion into my family.

"The Rattlesnake"

The Robot's wife came from a very ordinary working-class background. The Rattlesnake was uneducated, unattractive, with nothing special to offer when she darkened our door for the first time. She had bad skin, protruding teeth and greasy hair. But what she lacked in aesthetic appearance was replaced with unquestionable ambition. Her awkward body was flaunted in tight miniskirts and she was very willing to walk over others to get what she wanted. She gave off an air of sleazy arrogance and entitlement. A woman of poor character, driven only by her motivation to be seen as important. The Rattlesnake did not hide her vicious nature, she was proud of it, hissing, sneering and judging everyone in her path.

The Robot and Rattlesnake moved into our home after they got married. This was a temporary arrangement whilst their own house was being built. Mammy had several children and me as an infant at the time. Space was tight at home, but the Robot and his wife were accommodated and given their own room. Mammy's children were crammed together, sleeping in any available space. The Robot was often away with work, leaving the Rattlesnake with an opportunity to slither her way deeper and deeper into our family. With objective hindsight, it is not that surprising that Rattlesnake immediately gravitated towards Daddy. His dominant and ruthless character was attractive to her. In many ways, she admired his behaviour and wanted to be close to such a man. The fact that he was married, twice her age and her father-in-law was irrelevant.

The relationship between Daddy and the Rattlesnake started off pretending to be innocent on the surface. Going to church together on Sunday had all the hallmarks of a respectable family outing. This was a crude distraction to create an opportunity for a very private drive together afterwards. As the relationship developed, Daddy and the Rattlesnake went shopping without Mammy. They pretended that this domestic arrangement was to help my "stupid" mother to manage the housekeeping. They made her feel that she lacked the intelligence to add up the prices in the shop. The Rattlesnake was given full control of the weekly housekeeping money. This was the only thing that Mammy was allowed to manage in her humble little world. Now she had to beg my father's live in mistress for every penny and justify her reasons.

Mammy became a slave in her own home because she was scared that her children would suffer if she fought back. The Rattlesnake was pushing Mammy into the ground, slowly killing her and she was delighted that everyone could see her achievement. Daddy and the Rattlesnake were visibly energised when they were together, giggling and flirting, like naughty teenagers. Mammy was forced to go for long walks with her children to provide her abusers with some time to be alone. Explicit orders were given to stay away for several hours and Mammy was encouraged to comply with some money for sweets and cigarettes.

To escape from this hell, Mammy walked her children and smoked some cigarettes to find some comfort for a little while. The only way she could protest against the affair was to sleep on the sofa in the front room. She needed to maintain her dignity to survive this betrayal and keep some level of sanity. Daddy was not allowed to have her body whilst he was having sex with the Rattlesnake. The Robot did not react, perhaps he quietly blamed his father or he just believed the lie. Any form of demonstrations from within the family was met with aggression. The affair continued in plain view.

When the Robot and the Rattlesnake were ready to move into their newly built home, Daddy suddenly cut off his mistress. He had taken what he wanted and he probably became concerned that the affair would become public knowledge. He cast her aside, but a connection remained between them that would resurface in later years. The Robot and the Rattlesnake had children and they tried to glaze over the affair and move on. Perversely, they positioned themselves as an aspirational couple who should be admired publicly. Their new home was decorated with precision and symmetry, a middle-class show house with expensive furniture and modern appliances. But their marriage was a grand delusion and they both knew it.

Mammy told me about the affair when I was a small boy. She was talking to herself and partly confiding in me when we were alone. Perhaps she believed that I would not retain the information because I was so young. The ugly facts and her pain did register with me, but my idolisation of my father stopped me from consciously accepting the truth. But I was reminded of the existence of the affair every time Daddy and the Robot came close to being in the same space at the same time. Instinctively, I knew that they needed to be kept apart, without fully acknowledging the reason behind this tension. The rotten smell of betrayal also made me hate the Rattlesnake without question and I took every opportunity to irritate her. I could see her mocking Mammy, openly sniggering at my mother's humble demeanour, second-hand clothes and tattered handbag. The Rattlesnake developed a reciprocal hatred for me, she knew I was a threat and she aimed to keep me down.

"Forced Silence"

After the affair was over, Daddy needed to tidy up any residue and guarantee that the subject would not be discussed again. His first move was to threaten Mammy that he would leave her and go to England, but this was a bluff. He had no intention of leaving and he knew that running away would only point to his guilt. He also knew the financial implications of moving to England, he had a good salary in Ireland, no mortgage and more than one pension coming in. He simply denied any wrongdoing without blinking an eye and continued as normal. Mammy was completely broken and she knew that he would go to any length to make sure that the affair was buried. Daddy planned a way to show her exactly what he was capable of.

One night very late, Daddy suddenly announced that he wanted Mammy to come with him for a drive to help him with something. No clear explanation was provided, he just ordered her to the car and drove into the countryside. He didn't speak a word whilst he drove, deliberately keeping her guessing about the destination and his motivations. A few miles away from home Daddy suddenly stopped next to an old rubbish dump on a deserted country road. He got out of the car without a single word, left Mammy inside and disappeared into the darkness. Mammy was frozen with fear, her mind was racing, preparing for the worst. He returned after several minutes carrying the frame of an old wooden bed. He asked Mammy to help him load it into the boot, she was scared to get out of the car but she did what he asked. He then drove her home in complete silence. He didn't physically touch her, he didn't threaten her, but the message was clear. This level of psychological terror frightened Mammy into deep submission.

5. The Rebel

Our home was a tense and miserable place, nobody talked, no eye contact, like strangers drifting through an unwelcome space. My siblings learned to avoid Daddy, filtering him out when they could, sidestepping his traps, judgements and attacks. The easiest way to protect yourself from him was to simply make sure that you were not at home. In my role as Daddy's right-hand man, I was moulded into a tool that could be used to intimidate the family. Daddy encouraged my boyish aggression and he was visibly pleased as my physical strength developed as a teenager. I was given the authority to be hostile and use cutting verbal assaults to support his anti-family regime.

This role obviously complicated relations with my siblings.

It is now obvious to me that my father's tyranny negatively impacted my sisters' lives in particular. Any feminine or creative behaviour was an absolute no-go in our home. Mammy was not allowed to have proper mother-and-daughter relationships. My sisters witnessed their mother being abused and they were not protected from the bad men that came into their lives. Unsurprisingly, my sisters were not around that much. They all suffered through abusive relationships and they kept their painful experiences to themselves. If they ever asked for help, Daddy would only add to their problems by ridiculing them for their misfortunate choices.

"The Rebel"

My sisters were like aliens to me when I was growing up. There was no relationship because I did not know how to interact with them as women. However, one sister must be part of this story, because without her help, I may not have faced the truth about my father. The Rebel left school early and enjoyed a busy social life as a young woman. A sensitive and caring soul with a big heart, always thinking of others. Mammy needed her help with the children who came after her. The Rebel had to learn how to change nappies, cook and take care of small children when she was just a young girl herself.

I can remember benefiting many times as a child from the gifts that the Rebel bought for me. She was angry at Daddy and she was not always compliant to his tyrannical regime. Regular protests were staged by pursuing normal family rituals. At birthdays and Christmas, she always tried to do something small with her limited resources. In return for her kindness within the family, Daddy rejected her in a very obvious way and without any explanation for his decision. This dismissal and neglect really hurt the Rebel, and she waited for a chance to get the upper hand later in life.

The Rebel knew how to stand up for herself. Sometimes she fought back against Daddy with words, and sometimes she fought back with fists. I witnessed Daddy beating her up many times when she would not back down and accept his domination. These confusing clashes were like watching drunken men fighting outside a pub late at night. Dramatic and violent battles with screaming and wild lunges. Part of me wanted to support Daddy to maintain order as his right-hand man. But there was also a subdued part of me that knew he was wrong and the Rebel had a good reason to fight back. My loyalty to my father got in the way of doing the right thing and I have always felt guilty that I did not do more to protect my sister.

I was at home with Daddy and Mammy one evening. We were in the kitchen together, acting like a "mini-family", separated from the rest. I was often the buffer, entertaining Daddy, which allowed Mammy to relax for a little while. This created a temporary state of calm that would not be possible if other members of the family were present. Daddy was never happy with peace, and he started yet another pointless argument with Mammy. He complained that the Rebel was living with us and not paying her way. Daddy was shouting, knowing that the Rebel could hear him from her bedroom located at end of the long hallway. He repeatedly called her a "lazy bitch". Mammy was trying to calm him down, but it was too late, the fight was on.

The Rebel came out of her room to shout back and let Daddy know that she was not going to be intimidated. She told him that she hated him and she wished he was dead so that she could "spit on his grave". Shouting from both of them progressed into threats, and threats turned into a physical confrontation. Daddy grabbed the Rebel by the hair, pulling her up and down the hallway violently. He then administered hard slaps to her face with his heavy hands to break her resistance. But the Rebel fought back, his strikes to her face did not work and they struggled and grappled in the hallway. All I could hear was the high-pitched screams from the Rebel and aggressive grunts from Daddy, as he delivered each slap to her face with increasing force. Mammy was paralysed, crying and praying, she looked at me and her eyes told me to do something.

The fight escalated and crashed into the kitchen. I managed to intervene and separate Daddy and the Rebel, holding him back, whilst my sister continued to goad him and come after him. Daddy then grabbed the kettle from the range cooker to use as a weapon against his daughter. He tried to throw the boiling water but I managed to stop him just in time. I grabbed his arms to control his movement, tried to reason with him and I took the kettle out of his hands and placed it out of reach. He then said, “Patrick, tell her to back off, or I will take the kettle to her”. I had to stand between Daddy and the Rebel to stop the battle, holding my arms out in both directions to maintain distance, like a referee separating the amped-up fighters in a bad-tempered boxing match. Somehow, I managed to push the Rebel back into her room to create separation. I was the young bouncer in my home that night and Mammy was thankful that I was there to help.

Shouting continued from both of them at a distance, but the physical confrontation was over, for now. Daddy gave the Rebel a deadline to leave the house, he told Mammy repeatedly “I want her out of here”. Daddy knew that he had an ace card and he ordered her expulsion within two weeks. The Rebel responded from her room, telling him that she did not care, but she was deeply hurt by his physical and emotional assault. Daddy retreated to the kitchen, satisfied with his victory. The deadline that he imposed for the Rebel to leave was ignored, she would not let him bully her. I was vigilant and waiting for another fight, but the Rebel kept her distance and Daddy backed off temporarily. He knew that he could pick his moment again in the future. He never let anything go.

6. Happy Christmas

When the start of December arrived in our home every year, Daddy's anger level ramped up progressively on a daily basis. He made it clear that he was unwilling to tolerate any form of celebration. In his words, "Christmas is cancelled". As soon as the 1st of January arrived, Daddy changed his mood back to his regular level of hostility. The festive season was over and he had successfully denied his family. However, the Rebel always put up a Christmas tree and some basic decorations in our front room. Daddy tolerated this protest because the presence of a tree meant that our neighbours would see the coloured lights through the window as they walked past. This deception supported his fake public image as a family man in the village.

Christmas 1988 was memorable in a special way. It was Friday evening and the next day was Christmas Eve, but there was no food in the fridge and definitely no presents wrapped with love under the tree. Unexpectedly, my father did not come home after work at his usual time of 5 pm, he stayed on to have a drink with the men before they broke up until the new year. He was good at pretending to be social when necessary, but he very rarely drank alcohol because he worried that his mask would slip. Mammy and I were waiting at home, wondering why he was late and if we would have the chance to buy some food before Christmas day. This specific anxiety was later proved to be the least of our problems.

Daddy arrived home around 7 pm and he was very drunk. He walked into the house in a strange and agitated mood. I had never seen my father drunk before and I had no idea how to behave around him. He moved around the house, refusing to sit down and he began to bang his fist on the wall. He was making strange and muttered inward statements to himself. Mammy and I stayed with him initially, trying to calm him down and understand what he needed. Something was boiling and festering under the surface. I took the responsible role and followed Daddy into the backyard as he became more and more agitated. Mammy watched on, but she stayed back at a safe distance. Suddenly, Daddy erupted violently and started to smash anything in his way, breaking glass, picking up heavy objects and throwing them with wild aggression.

He was possessed, grunting and growling, taking out his rage on everything in his path.

This sudden eruption terrified Mammy, she got out of the house fast and ran away. I just stood silently watching him, waiting for it to stop so that I could help him. I can remember being very practical, taking obstacles and hazards out of his way as he smashed through the backyard. Daddy's violent exertions eventually made him tired and he stopped to catch his breath. He was panting and holding his head in his hands. He did not look at me or speak to me, but I felt that he wanted me to stay. He then retreated to the bathroom and started to wash his face with cold water, trying to sober up, realising that he had lost control temporarily.

Unfortunately, the drama was not contained and came to the attention of the Robot and the Rattlesnake. They pretended that they cared for Mammy and the family, but they had their own agenda. The Robot decided to confront his father, this was a bad idea with violent potential. They had not been in the same space for many years after the affair with the Rattlesnake ended. I was standing in the backyard when the Robot arrived to face his father. He approached purposefully, Daddy was still standing in the bathroom facing the mirror, washing his face with cold water. The tension was very high and the slightest irritation could set him off again.

The Robot took a position in the bathroom doorway and immediately started to lecture his father. He started his speech with a very telling opening line, he said

“We have got you now”. Daddy was told that he was going to be condemned to a psychiatric institution for his abuse of the family. The Robot laid it on thick and didn’t stop for a breath. Daddy ignored him, he did not want to acknowledge his presence or validate his accusations. He said “go away”, several times over and continued to wash his face with cold water. Several warnings were given, but the Robot couldn’t stop himself, this was his moment.

Suddenly, Daddy turned and moved to attack and silence this annoyance. The Robot screamed in shock and terror and quickly dived through the kitchen door to escape the blows. He managed to get the door closed and he pulled some furniture across to hold it, but it would not last very long. Daddy attacked the door with his fists initially, but then he grabbed an iron bar from the backyard and he began to break down the door. I was standing close by, watching, listening and feeling the conflict. The iron bar smashed the surface of the wooden kitchen door, but Robot was able to hold the door closed. Daddy needed a better plan and he was going to up the stakes in this violent confrontation.

Daddy went out to the backyard and returned with a chainsaw to get through the door, he was determined to reach his target. Whilst he was trying to get the chainsaw going and preoccupied, the Robot computed that he was in mortal danger and made an exit through the kitchen window. Daddy realised that he was getting away and gave chase through our garden with the chainsaw in hand. Luckily, the Robot was fast enough to escape unharmed. Daddy returned to the house, went inside and calmly took his usual seat in the smashed-up kitchen to collect his thoughts.

At this stage of the incident, I wanted to check where Mammy was. I found her down the road with the Rattlesnake, frozen with fear. Mammy did not know what to do next and she was too afraid to go back to the house. The Rebel was walking home that night and she came across the drama. Mammy told her what happened, but she wanted to see it for herself. She entered our home and walked carefully through the debris like she was walking through a crime scene. Daddy was in the kitchen, just sitting there silently, he did not even look at her as she walked past. He was now thinking about how he could get out of the situation. The Rebel got out of the house fast, unnerved by his cold silence. She returned to the safe zone to join Mammy and other members of the family.

My instinct was to go back to the house and help Daddy, but my good intentions were interrupted. The Rattlesnake was energised by the conflict between Daddy and the Robot, she knew that they were fighting over her. She told me to go to a reliable neighbour up the road to phone the police. She avoided this task herself to ensure she was not connected with the act of reporting my father to the law. In the confusion, I followed her direction, I went to the reliable neighbour and he called the police immediately. This neighbour had a son the same age as me, we went to school together. My schoolmate watched me crying in their kitchen and trying to explain what had happened. I could see in his eyes that he felt sorry for me.

The reliable neighbour then asked me to come with him to see Daddy, I think he was nervous and he wanted me with him to justify his reason for entering our house. He approached cautiously, opened the gate and he called out for Daddy, but there was no response. We walked together into the backyard, and Daddy was there, standing and staring coldly into space. The neighbour made some small talk, but he got no response from Daddy. He quickly made his excuses, left me with Daddy and went back to the safety of his own home and family. I am sure my dysfunctional family was the topic of conversation during their Christmas dinner that year.

Whilst I was with the reliable neighbour, the Rattlesnake also somehow managed to manipulate the

Rebel to call the local doctor to report Daddy's psychotic behaviour. Once again, in the confusion, the Rebel followed her instruction. The Rattlesnake was trying to secure the correct official authority to condemn Daddy. Maybe this was revenge because he cut her off and she wanted to eradicate their ugly affair. If she couldn't have him, she wanted him out of sight so that she could exoncrate herself. Or maybe she thought that she could seize more power and dominate my family with him out of the way. There was so much going on that night that I was not ready to understand as a 13-year-old. The adults were having hushed-up conversations in little splinter groups, but when I asked what was going on, they just looked away.

"Cover-Up"

The police were on their way and Daddy knew he had to cover his tracks. Despite his severely drunken state, he drove his car a couple of miles into the countryside to avoid a drunk driving charge. I went with him and we walked home together at a fast pace. He needed to get back before the police arrived and manage the conversation. As we walked that dark country road together, he was talking to himself, rehearsing his excuses and getting ready to deny everything. I remember that I was reassuring him and trying to calm him. In my childish way, I wanted to protect him and support him through the crisis. He went straight to bed when we arrived home without saying a single word to anyone. Tension was high, he was hiding in the bedroom with the door firmly closed, licking his wounds, daring anyone to enter and challenge him.

The doctor arrived first. However, he only agreed to see Daddy if the police were present. The police eventually showed up and they went into the bedroom without the doctor to assess the situation. We all waited in the hallway, Mammy was silent and her body language was very nervous, she knew that she would be questioned. Daddy told the police that his outburst was due to the death of his mother several years back, he did idolise his fierce mother but this was a distraction to gain sympathy. Daddy knew that this excuse would seem plausible. The police came out of the bedroom shaking their heads and shrugging their shoulders, they believed his lie and they could see no crime.

The doctor then went into the bedroom to see Daddy, whilst the police were instructed to wait. He was in there for some time, my father was gifted at putting on the charm when required. Once again, he put all the blame on being drunk and grieving for his mother. The doctor came out of the bedroom to talk to the family, but, he was concerned and troubled, something did not sit right with him. The doctor then said, "he is either he is a psychopath or a very good liar". At that time, I had no idea what a psychopath was and I was unwilling to have a negative view of my father. The police and the doctor asked Mammy if she felt safe to be with Daddy, hoping that she would give them what they needed, but she looked away and kept her silence. Despite the violence and our smashed home that night, Mammy accepted her tyrannical husband, as she did throughout her life.

Daddy stayed in the bedroom and out of sight that night, not willing to face his terrified family or acknowledge his actions. There were signs of a violent clash everywhere, holes in the doors, broken glass, splinters of wood on the floor and furniture knocked over. The Robot and the Rattlesnake kept their distance, they had both pushed their luck that night. Everyone was in shock and drained after the high of adrenaline. There was now a forced calm after the storm. In these times of chaos, some of my brothers and sisters seemed to come together, united in a crisis. A weird truce to put aside dysfunction and differences in an extreme situation. They knew deep down that there was a bigger problem than sibling conflict. Daddy was still in charge and recovering in bed.

"Cash Distraction"

There was a dark atmosphere hanging over the house the next morning. Mammy and my sisters were busy sweeping up the glass and trying to hide the reminders of the previous night. Daddy acted like nothing happened, but he wanted to buy my silence and continued loyalty. He drove me to the local town and I was given £30 cash. I explored the shops excitedly and bought a sports bag and some other boyish things. This generosity from my father on Christmas Eve was very unexpected, but his plan was effective. I brushed the whole episode under the carpet and I did not connect this violent night with my inability to enjoy Christmas as an adult. Mammy did her best to pull together a basic dinner from nothing that year, but the damage was done. Daddy ate his dinner alone and everyone stayed away from the house.

7. Running Away

As I moved through my teenage years, I found out that I was good at the Irish national sport Gaelic Football. Good enough to be on the local club team, the school team and eventually the County team. My name was in the regional newspaper many times when I played well in a match, I had talent. Some of the coaches really supported and recognised me, and made me feel good about myself. I must have played in a hundred Gaelic Football games in my teenage years and I can only remember Daddy going to a couple of games, and that was because it was a final and I begged him. I think that he only went to those games because he knew that it would make him look good in our local area. He was not interested in Gaelic football, so my passion was pointless to him.

Gaelic Football was my saviour as a teenager, it gave me a sense of belonging that was missing at home. I loved the bus journeys to the matches, loads of enthusiastic boys telling jokes and having a laugh. It felt like a family to me, somewhere where I was safe and valuable. It was a place that I could express myself and escape for a while. I have many sweet memories of calm and warm summer nights, training and playing games on lush green fields. Growing up with a group of boys, starting together with the under fourteen years team and progressing together as young men to the under sixteen and the under eighteen team. I learned about true brotherhood, loyalty and commitment. We won many matches and championships, being part of that team gave my life meaning. I am sure that I would have gone down the wrong path as a teenager if I did not have this exposure to sport.

"Hunting Girls"

The start of secondary school initiated my interest in girls and I made an immediate impact. I used to hang around town at lunch with the boys, posing and trying to catch the attention of the endless flow of girls pouring out from the nearby convent school. I started to notice that I was popular with girls. Shy teenage girls passed messages to me through friends to let me know they liked me. I got more attention than the boys around me and this new status felt good. I enjoyed the reward chemistry and my behaviour became focused on gaining more of this feel-good power. This was the early stage of my sexual awakening and I became completely tuned in.

There were local discos in little backward town halls every weekend. This was a chance to have a slow dance with girls, up close, touching, holding on whilst the romantic 80s power ballad songs were playing. Asking girls for dances, getting rejected sometimes, but mostly getting accepted. Taking them by the hand to the dancefloor in front of my friends was a huge boost to my boyhood confidence. Even at fourteen years old, I was often getting girls who were two years older than me and this put me in a different league compared to my boyhood peers. It became a game for me, hunting a target, winning a prize and then on to the next one. This became a compulsion for me and progressed into my adult life.

Going for a romantic walk by the river with a girl was a frequent activity. But if I met them in a local disco, I used to run away and hide. I was dumped too at times, but I brushed it off quickly and continued to invest in my growing ego. Pretty soon I had built up a reputation as a player. Whilst I was busy chasing girls, I did not have to sit with my own emotions and face the truth about my father. There was no way that I could allow real feelings of intimacy into my life. From what I witnessed at home, I didn't understand it and I didn't trust myself enough to believe it was possible.

"Drinking Problem"

I started drinking at thirteen years of age, and there were obvious signs of binging and addiction from the start. During one cold and frosty night in December, I was waiting for some friends in the town square before going to a school disco. I kept warm drinking whisky as a neat shot, pouring it into the bottle cap and necking it straight back. A half bottle of whisky quickly disappeared and I was dangerously drunk. By the time my friends arrived, I was out of control, stopping traffic on the busy road for fun. Some of my teachers were on the door to control entry to the disco that night. I stumbled up to the door, paid the fee and then crashed into the disco with a clumsy force. The teachers stared at me with disapproval, they knew I was drunk but I was still allowed to come in. I was looking for attention and my antics were talked about in school the following week. I wonder now exactly what the teachers discussed.

We left the school disco quickly and headed to a "nightclub". A club in rural Ireland was a hall in the middle of nowhere, filled with people from the surrounding villages and towns arriving in minibuses to dance the night away to Bryan Adams, The Cure, Madness and Guns & Roses. It was a mixture of farmers boasting about the size of their tractor and unemployed Punks and Mods stealing drinks and jackets. Our minibus arrived at the front of the club and I fell out and landed at the bouncer's feet. I had been going to local adult nightclubs for a while and all of the bouncers knew me, but I was not allowed to go inside that night. I was bundled into a taxi and dropped at the crossroads of my village, as I was too drunk to give the driver directions. He just pushed me out of the car onto the ground and drove off, I assume that someone paid him.

It was a frosty night, but I was warm from the whisky. In my drunken state, I decided to lie down at the side of the road to sleep for a while. Mammy went to see her friend for a smoke most nights, and as she was walking home she came across me stuck to the frozen ground and fast asleep. She managed to wake me up and get me to my feet. I stumbled home behind her, as she paused and waited patiently for me to catch up. I was in a very bad state and it must have worried her. If I had slept longer in that sub-zero temperature the consequences could have been serious. This would not be the last time that Mammy saved me from danger.

"London Calling"

I had an argument with the Rebel late one evening, for some silly reason that I can't even remember. My first instinct was to write a note to Mammy to inform her that I was leaving for good and I headed off without even packing a bag. I walked a few miles to the local town, still determined at this stage and ignoring my lack of preparation. The next stage was hitching a lift to Dublin without a thought of where I would go or stay for the night. After landing in central Dublin, I realised that I had no money and no options. A bench at Euston train station became my temporary accommodation for the night. It was cold and exposed, but I was tired and I managed to sleep. I was woken up in the early morning by some official-looking man who ordered me to move on.

Stupidly, I thought I could make a new start, get a job and then go further. But I was left walking around Dublin without purpose and very hungry. I eventually went to a police station in the afternoon and said that I had lost my wallet. The police officer wrote me a note that I used on the bus to get home. When I arrived home in the evening with my tail between my legs, to my surprise, nobody noticed that I had run away. The emotional leaving home note that I had written to Mammy was still in the same place and untouched. It was just a matter of time before I would make a more successful attempt. If I had any money in my pocket that night, I know that I would have gone further and never come back.

"Vauxhall Part 1"

When I was fifteen years old I met a girl from London. She was visiting relatives in our local village and I noticed her immediately. She was eighteen, petite, pretty, with short black spiky hair and Spanish looks. Her fashion was the UK rave scene, luxury sportswear, baggy jeans, hooped earrings and Reebok trainers. She was very cool and from the future, a place where I badly wanted to go. Whilst she was visiting Ireland she was closely guarded by her cousin, who would not allow us to have any privacy to explore my teenage sexual motivations. We went for some walks, but the cousin was always there to intervene and bring an immediate stop to activity. She went back to London after the holiday, but she took my address and wrote to me over the next year. Her letters were romantic and stated one very important fact, that we were going to have sex, if I could get to London. I was a virgin and this opportunity to become a man motivated me to scramble together £100 spending money and make the necessary arrangements. I made my first solo trip to London during the next summer when I was sixteen.

I was inexperienced and young, but I was confident that I would be able to find my way around London. The ferry carried me from Dublin to North Wales, then I travelled to London on a coach, landing at Victoria Station. I did not know it yet, but I would make the exact same journey three years later to escape Ireland. The underground metro was navigated successfully to Vauxhall station and the final stage of my journey was a short bus ride. I had to call her home landline from a public phone box to receive explicit instructions on the correct bus stop to get off. This was suspicious and she was not acting as I expected. I had visions of her running to meet me at the train station with the love that she proclaimed in her letters, but she could not even be bothered to leave home. She was standing on the street when I got off the bus, but she was cold and made no eye contact. It felt like she was pretending that she did not know me.

We walked to the flat that she shared with her older brother and father. They lived in a high-rise block on a council estate, an inner-city place where you needed to be switched on. I must have looked like a complete green tourist. We left her flat straight away and hung around with her friend in a local park. Her friend was a cool girl, they smoked marijuana with experience and chatted about going out to raves and brushes with the police. I just sat there and tried to fit in but I must have looked like such an Irish country boy, these city girls were miles ahead of me. We sat together on the grass in that little park close to Vauxhall, I looked on and didn't contribute much to the conversation, I was in awe and out of my depth.

I had no experience with drugs back then, but things would change dramatically in the future. Jump ahead ten years, I would find myself in Vauxhall again and very committed to the clubs and drugs scene. I was destined to become a very different person in the future.

Someone who would be very familiar with many kinds of drugs, Ecstasy, GHB, Ketamine, Cocaine. That teenage Irish boy was replaced by a wild man, all weekend parties, hunting for action and thrills. Vauxhall became a strange magnetic location for me three times in my life. I always seemed to land there when I was lost or at times of significant change.

Things did not work out with my holiday romance and I only stayed a couple of days. I had built up the whole thing into some kind of super serious "having sex ceremony". I had rehearsed when and how to put the condom on, my game was mechanical and obviously inexperienced. When it was time to leave, my holiday romance and her friend took me to Vauxhall station and drove away quickly. Ironically, I did lose my virginity later that summer to an English girl visiting Ireland to see relatives. I met her in a disco and we had an extremely unerotic encounter in a haybarn located conveniently in a nearby farmyard. Discos and farmyards in close proximity was not that rare in rural Ireland back then. It was awkward and not what I expected, but this started my journey and compulsion for instant sex.

"Court Case"

I was certainly no angel during my teenage years and I did my fair share of anti-social activity. However, my delinquent juvenile behaviour was not driven by anger or rage. My motivation was more about impressing peers and chasing excitement. There were dangerous boys in the area who were highly destructive young men. They had no fear of the police and went to prison many times. I did my best to avoid them because I knew that they would force me into serious criminal activity to be accepted. They scared me and I was on the wrong side of their casual daily violence a couple of times. To be in their gang was an attractive prospect, gaining status and notoriety across the county, but I lacked their vicious nature.

However, I did manage to get myself into some trouble with the law. I had a persistent battle with three stupid boys from my local area. The usual teenage scuffles, name-calling, push and shove, but it never went too far. One of these boys was distinctive by his large physicality. He was fat and certainly fancied his chances of beating me up. Whenever we came across each other, he always postured up and made various elaborate promises about what he was going to do to me. But nothing ever came of his threats, it was just big talk from a safe distancc.

One afternoon, I was helping my father to build a stone wall at the front of our house. The three boys were standing on the road directly opposite, maybe ten meters away, banded together in their little gang. They were laughing and sniggering at me and they were not trying to hide it. It was a direct provocation, but I ignored them and continued working, mixing cement and carrying large stones as instructed. Daddy could see that I was frustrated but ordered me not to respond several times. After a tense and restrained hour or so Daddy eventually broke his silence and said "fuck off home or I will let Patrick off".

This was an unusual statement when I think about it now. I was being described as some kind of tool that could be used to attack on command. The fat boy responded first and said: “Fuck off old cunt”. This was a mistake.

Without thinking or giving any warning, I charged across the road and grabbed the fat boy by the scruff of his jacket. The other boys scattered and ran to safety. The fat one was less fortunate, he was straddling a bike and he struggled to get away from me. He tried to hit me but I was ready and I delivered his punishment. In the exchange, he got punched in the face repeatedly by my enthusiastic right arm. I fucking hammered him and his friends did not come to his aid. After the short fight was over, the fat boy picked himself up and proceeded to cycle home. But as he rode away into the distance, he thought it was clever to shout back more abuse aimed at Daddy and me. This was his second mistake.

I sprinted after my target and pulled him off his bike, covering the distance in seconds. Several men were watching the drama unfold on the road, the fight was stopping the traffic. I was eventually peeled off him and he was sent away in a badly beaten condition, his face looked like he had been in a car accident. He went home and played the victim to his parents. The police were called, but I anticipated this and I made sure I was not home when they came looking for me. But it was just a matter of time before I would have to answer to the law. Formal statements were taken from all parties by the police, I stated self-defence and they blamed me, forgetting to mention their provocation. A court date was set and we were all ready for a public show.

Daddy came to court with me when the day arrived. The courthouse was packed and there were many cases for the judge to hear. As I sat waiting for my turn, I felt very vulnerable watching the other cases unfold. The police testified and the defendants were taken away to jail when they were found guilty. I leaned close to my father and I said: "I'm scared". Without even looking at me, he said "Don't fuck this up" in a very angry voice and he stared straight ahead in stern silence. In my family, it is always better to deal with problems yourself, compared to having his contempt added on top. The three stupid boys were in court, dressed up in badly fitted shirts and cheap ties. They sat together, avoiding eye contact with me but I could see them grinning and giggling, anticipating their victory. They were waiting for the moment that I would be taken away in handcuffs like a most wanted criminal.

They testified against me that day, exaggerating my aggression and forgetting to mention their role in the confrontation. I stuck to my story, I was defending myself when I was threatened. To my surprise, the case was quickly dismissed with no conviction against me. Irish jails were full and the judge had more serious criminals to deal with. The three stupid boys were standing in the car park afterwards with perplexed faces like they had just lost something but they couldn't figure out exactly what. I walked up to them calmly, held out my wrists and said: "Look at my handcuffs, they are taking me away to jail". I laughed and walked off.

The fight caused a scandal in the village and I was the source of gossip. The Rattlesnake was energised by this little episode. As the court date approached, she was grinning from ear to ear if we came across each other. She was hoping that I would be humiliated and sentenced to jail. I was told that the Rattlesnake drove the boys who witnessed the fight and ran away to court that day. She wanted to make sure that they testified against me and that I was punished in public. The fact that I was not convicted must have really irritated her.

"Exam Results"

After five years of secondary school, my final exams arrived in the summer of 1993, I was eighteen years old. Most of my siblings did not finish secondary school, they dropped out and they were the targets of Daddy's scorn because of their lack of academic success. I had the intelligence to get through the lessons and navigate school successfully, but I was an average student. Daddy took no interest in my progress and I did not know the direction to go that would please him. The exam results were released during the summer break, we knew the date and every student waited anxiously. On the morning the results were made available, all the boys in my year gathered in little nervous groups outside the school walls, waiting for the official brown envelope with our printed names to be handed over. The outcome would point to a couple of potential options. A place in college or university, or the end of academic life.

My geography teacher came out with the envelopes stacked in his hands and all the boys stiffened themselves when they saw him. He was a large man, with scruffy grey hair, thick glasses and a booming voice that carried a long distance. My name was called, I approached cautiously, he looked me in the eyes, handed over the envelope and gave me a half smile. I walked away and immediately ripped it open with excitement, trying to take in all the information at once. Actually, I had achieved respectable results and I had enough points to get a place in college. Mammy was alone when I arrived home. She smiled and beamed with pride when I showed her the small piece of paper with my results. However, she spotted one small problem, there was a chink in my armour. I got an E Grade in the Irish Gaelic language.

I waited anxiously for Daddy to come home from work. Mammy was hanging around in the background, staying close to me, she knew an attack was imminent and she was ready to comfort me afterwards. I heard the door open, there was a long silence, then Daddy walked into the kitchen in his usual hostile mood. I was feeling enthusiastic and joyful, hoping that I would be congratulated for my good results. I passed the piece of paper to my father optimistically. He took a quick look and then threw my results on the table dismissively. His only comment as he walked out of the room was "I told you that you would fail Irish". He cut me down in one move and I took the blow.

"College Life"

I started college in Dublin in 1993 when I was eighteen years old. I picked business studies as my chosen diploma because I believed that Daddy would approve of that direction, but I found it very boring. Anything creative would not have been tolerated and didn't enter my mind. The college grant system was means-tested based on your parent's financial circumstances, so I had no grant money. The start of every month was a repetitive ordeal, begging for the train fare and any materials required. I could not even afford the bus to carry me to college from the train station when I arrived in Dublin. The six-mile round trip was walked every day, rain or shine. Mammy made me cheese sandwiches for lunch and I washed them down with a litre of milk to fill me up as cheaply as possible. Sitting in the college canteen was depressing, watching the other students having a cooked lunch and meeting up for a coffee or planning a beer after class. They were enjoying student life and I was on the outside looking in.

I felt the pressure of going to college because I was the only member of my family to make it beyond secondary school. I had at least three years ahead of me living this basic life if I wanted to get a diploma, and even longer if I wanted a degree. It was hard and I was not motivated, something was missing from the whole experience. The classes were uninspiring, I was sleepwalking through the college experience. My day started at 6 am, catching a lift to the train station from a local man going to town. Then the train to Dublin, walk to college, classes all day and a long walk back to the station to take the train home. My year one exams were passed successfully, I was a model student, but I did not feel connected to what I was doing. This was the calm before the storm. A slow and quiet drift was building under the surface. I did not know it yet, but I was starting to float away towards new waters and very soon my life in Ireland would be out of sight.

"City Boy"

At the end of my first year in college, I got a job in security and started to live in Dublin over the summer months of 1994. I rented a small house just off the north circular road for £30 per week. There was a very good reason why it was vacant and cheap. It was located in an extremely socially deprived and dangerous area. Back then, Dublin was not the 21st-century cosmopolitan city that it is now. There were still many “no-go” areas populated by tough inner-city people living a life of daily crime. The outside of my rented house resembled a jail. There was a large steel door, multiple locks, metal bars on all the windows and loops of barbed wire on the roof. The inside looked like an abandoned home, it smelled damp, with hardly any furniture and nothing worked properly. But this humble little house was all mine and I loved it for what it represented, freedom and independence.

At night, I could hear hardened kids on the streets in gangs and up to no good. Shouting, swearing, breaking glass and sometimes lighting fires. Any cars that stopped at the traffic lights on the main road were vulnerable to being robbed. The kids grabbed anything valuable by forcing car doors open or reaching through open windows. There was a local shop on the corner and I sometimes went there to get bread or milk late at night. Locking my bike outside was pointless. I had to bring the bike inside and hold on to it, otherwise it would be stolen by the kids in the blink of an eye. The locals knew that I was not one of them, they spotted me a mile away, but I kept my head down and I didn't judge them. I was not inner-city class, but I was harmless enough to be accepted by them.

At some point over the summer, I went home to my village to catch up with friends. On Sunday evening before I returned to Dublin, Mammy begged Daddy to drive me back to my little rented house, she wanted to see where and how I was living. As we got closer, her face changed, her motherly instincts were proved right. Mammy was shocked by how rough the area was and my jail-like house. She came inside to look around but said very little. I tried to be positive and enthusiastic about my life in Dublin, but she went home deeply worried. Daddy just sneered and said that my adventure would "teach me a lesson".

Dublin life gave me a new rhythm. Off to work early in the morning on my bike to stand as a security guard all day outside some corporate building. Completing long shifts professionally and happy to have a basic wage. My earnings were around £8K per year and I thought that was close to my upper level. My supervisors and managers seemed to have amazing jobs, company car and a salary of maybe £20K per year. This was a level beyond my reach. But around ten years later and much to my surprise, I would become head of security for a large company and earn close to £100K per year at one stage of my career. Position and money are not the measures of people, but I did not realise I could be a leader. Daddy ensured that I did not develop authentic confidence and I needed to break from him to become more.

My Friday salary payment was an opportunity to go shopping every week. I always got a buzz from spending money and I used to treat myself to a cheap meal out. Looking back now, this behaviour was sad, sitting in a pizza restaurant on my own to celebrate in isolation. We were conditioned by Daddy to conceal any money or sense of joy, he was always on hand to remind us that we did not deserve to feel good. This emotional behaviour with money became a consistent pattern throughout my adult life. Any sudden cash injection became an immediate spend and a feel-good opportunity. A guilty secret that made me progressively more and more reckless as the amounts of cash increased.

"All or Nothing"

Now I can see that I have been a loner at many points in my life. I didn't have any friends in Dublin and I went out on my own mostly. Nights out were filled with knocking back drinks and having sex with random girls in the drunken chaos. Clubs that were packed and noisy were good for me, nobody would notice that I was there alone. I could move from a sudden decision to have a drink, to being very drunk and acting recklessly in a short period. Once I had the first shot I was off like a rocket, animated, pushing buttons and taking risks, stomping around in a drunken state. I had a "fuck it" attitude and I pretended to myself that this was fun, but it was sad and dangerous. My childhood environment created a hard-wired pattern of all-or-nothing behaviour and a sniff of alcohol seemed to grab me and take me on a wild journey.

My drunken antics sometimes brought me attention that I did not want. Young men who wanted to punch me in the face for misbehaving or stealing girls that they were interested in. I was aware that I pissed them off, but I would deliberately stand close to them, daring them to attack. Luckily, I managed to avoid any serious assaults.

Some young inner-city men carried knives and screwdrivers in those times. Pushing the wrong person would result in a nasty hole in me. Frustration and loneliness were coming to the surface every time I had a drink. Making a life in Dublin was incomplete. I was searching for something new and it would not be long before I would force a dramatic change.

"Tension Building"

At the end of the summer of 1994, I moved back home with Daddy and Mammy. This felt like stepping backwards in time. The plan at that stage was three more years of college, but living at home again was immediately strained and uncomfortable, something had changed. I was a now nineteen-year-old man, bigger, stronger and more independent. However, Daddy still required me to continue as his little boy helper. He gave me orders, I pushed back and we had a few minor arguments, but nothing that escalated into a full-blown confrontation. Mammy was worried, she could see the change in me and she could feel the tension building.

Waiting for college to start again in early October was painfully slow. I kept my head down and I left the house as much as possible to avoid Daddy and keep the peace. Finally, the day arrived to return to college and I travelled to Dublin enthusiastically, meeting back up with the other students was something to look forward to. However, after a few short classes to introduce the new year we were told that we had no further lectures for the next two days, this was not good news. Daddy was waiting for any opportunity to put me in my place and I knew that there would be unbearable tension if I was hanging around at home. The stage was set for a fight with my tyrannical father.

The following morning, I deliberately got out of Daddy's way. I went for a walk in the vast fields behind the house with a friend and our dogs. Walking with the dogs was always a great way to relax, I loved it. My friend and I spent as long as possible on the walk, but eventually, we had to head back. As we approached my friend's house, we noticed that a farmer had cut the trees and hedges. There was loads of free firewood to be taken by any locals who wanted it. Many Irish village homes had open fires, range cookers or stoves and this was a bonus for those lucky enough to spot the opportunity.

My friend was a down-to-earth and humble guy, he worked hard and he had to play a big role supporting his own family. I decided to help him to carry the free firewood into his yard. We grabbed the abundant branches and large blocks of wood that were laid out everywhere in the field, loaded them onto a wheelbarrow and moved them the short distance to his yard. We returned to the field repeatedly to grab as much as possible, but helping my friend was going to irritate someone.

Daddy suddenly entered the field in his car with a large trailer attached. He was well organised to take full advantage of the situation. Word had gotten around quickly and it was first come, first serve. When he saw that I was helping my friend he immediately became jealous. How dare I help another and not be available to serve his needs. He got out of his car, looked at me with anger and said; “You have turned out to be a right little bollocks”. This attack was unprovoked from my perspective, I was hurt, but I was not going to lie down this time. I fired back instantly, “Well, that’s lovely, coming from you”. I thought that my sarcastic response would wound him, but my words went nowhere. He just looked away with disgust and dismissed me.

“Sudden Departure”

Something snapped inside of me. I left the field immediately, walked home and went straight to my bedroom. I was cursing and swearing to myself as I packed a bag quickly. Mammy was at home and she stood by watching me. She asked "Where are you going?", and I responded, "Anywhere to get away from him". I was always impulsive and quick-tempered, but this was different. Daddy had run out of people to beat up, everyone had left home and I was his next target. I was so animated that I didn't even take the time to look at Mammy's face properly. Her youngest child was leaving home in front of her eyes, and there was nothing she could do to stop it.

We had several dogs at home back then, but one special terrier was mine. He was white with brown patches, a sweet soul and I made him feel like a hero when we walked in the fields together. The dogs usually stuck together in a pack at the back of the house, but he seemed to be concerned that I was upset. He followed me to the gate and stared at me intensely, he was saying goodbye. I was in such a hurry to go that I did not even look at Mammy as I pushed through the gate and walked down the road. As I made my way to the local town about three miles away, I was upset, but I was also kind of relieved in a weird way. Something told me that this argument with Daddy was a gift, and I knew that I was never coming back.

The bank in town was my first stop. I withdrew all of the cash I had saved for my second year at college. The cashier handed me £300 and I stuffed the notes deeply into my jacket pocket, hoping that I could make it last as long as possible. I bought a ticket for the ferry from Dublin to Holyhead in north Wales for the next morning, plus a coach ride to take me to London. The bus carried me to Dublin that afternoon and I found a cheap hostel for the night. There was not a single ounce of doubt about the outcome of my plan. I did not want to turn back because I knew that I would have to face Daddy. There was something very final about the situation and I was certain that it was better to take a risk and run away. I went to sleep that night thinking about a new life in England.

The next day started with a beautiful autumn morning. As I boarded the ferry at Dublin port, there was a clear blue sky and everything felt so crisp and alive. I went out on deck to look back at the land that I was leaving behind as we crossed the Irish Sea. I was trying to be positive, talking to myself and making grand plans about an independent life, but the facts and reality were very different. I had limited money, nowhere to go, no job and no friends. The severity of the situation was now starting to slowly penetrate my thoughts. A sense of loneliness started to creep in when I landed in North Wales and boarded the coach to London. I tried to strike up a conversation with two girls sitting close to me on the coach, but it was forced and desperate. I was on my own with no real plan or place to go.

8. New Start

The coach arrived at Victoria station at around 11 pm on a Friday night. The place was completely empty and hollow. Shops and cafes were locked behind cold metal shutters, there were virtually no people around and I had no idea what to do next. Sleeping rough was not a good option, I needed to find somewhere cheap for the night. Luckily, I stumbled across a little kiosk just outside the station advertising a hostel. The lady sitting in the kiosk took my cash fee for a single night but then informed me that the hostel was not local and that a minibus would come to transport me to the location somewhere in the city.

I waited for the minibus with some other travellers, mostly a group of over-enthusiastic Australian young men, chatting excitedly about their adventures. Their obvious sense of brotherhood made me notice that I was on my own. We packed ourselves into the minibus when it arrived and we were carried for about five minutes through the bright lights of London. The roads were not that busy and I was taking in the big buildings, shop windows and rows of well-organised houses in side streets. This was no place for an aimless stranger like me. London was a serious and heartless city.

"Vauxhall Part 2"

The hostel appeared to be a former high-rise council block building converted into a super hostel with hundreds of beds. There was a bar and a pool table on the ground floor, with pumping music and a very strange crowd. Edgy people were lurking in corners of the bar, borderline homeless and junky types who were happy to have some shelter for the night. There were also groups of travellers looking for a cheap roof over their head and a dry bed. Some people were drunk and high on drugs, I felt a little unsafe and my instinct was to hide my cash in my underwear. That night I slept very lightly in an open dormitory and I was relieved to wake up on Saturday morning with my cash and possessions still intact.

As I walked away from the hostel that Saturday morning the area and buildings seemed familiar to me in the daylight. I stopped for a moment and I looked around to take in the landmarks. Coincidentally, the high-rise building where I had stayed in Vauxhall when I was visiting as a horny sixteen-year-old was very close by. I recognised the shops, local roads and the parks. Mysteriously, I was back in the very same part of London once again. I walked to the underground metro station and I smiled to myself. The twists and turns of life brought me back to Vauxhall again, and this would not be the last time that I would end up there during a turning point in my life.

The only familiar place I knew was a cousin on my mother's side who lived in an affluent town about one hour away by train. I had visited her three years before on my solo trip to London, but this time she was not aware that I was coming. Her posh husband did not like me and he ordered that I was only allowed to stay for two nights when I arrived unexpectedly on Saturday afternoon. He spoke like he was royalty and looked down on me as some stupid Irish savage. My cousin was a nice woman, but her hands were tied in this unhappy marriage. I sensed that I was not welcome, but I was glad to have a couple of nights' free accommodation and some time to plan.

Despite the uncertain start, I decided to stay in that English commuter town. It was different from both village life in Ireland and the big city of London. It was a kind of middle ground and I felt safe there. I got straight to business on Monday morning and I secured a small room in a shared house with an Italian landlord who was heavily invested in property. Every room in the house was rented individually to either a student looking for cheap accommodation or adults in an unenviable situation. There was no lounge or dining room, just the kitchen and bathroom were shared. I paid the deposit and one week's rent in advance, £100 in total. This left me with a very measured amount of cash to keep going. The dusty curtains from the window in my room were used to cover me on a bare mattress on my first night in my new home. I had nothing, but I was determined to move forward and make things better. No matter what, going back to Ireland was not an option.

"Emotional Letters"

I was working as a hotel porter within a few days, my financial status meant that I couldn't mess around. The job had low pay, but I could eat all the food that I wanted, which felt like a daily bonus. I knew that Mammy would be worried about me, so I made contact. She used the coin operated payphone in the local village pub to speak with me because there was no landline at home. It was better than way, I did not want Daddy to know about my communication with Ireland and Mammy. I also wrote many letters, telling Mammy about how I was going to make her proud and stating that I did not care about my father. It must have broken her heart reading those letters. Sometimes I added a £10 or £20 note to the letter as a surprise. Sending cash was difficult, it was more than I could afford. But I knew that she treasured the money for what it represented, a sign that I was still thinking of her. Those letters were saved in her cluttered handbag over the years to keep me close.

"Psycho House 1"

Unfortunately, I soon discovered that the room I rented was not a secure place to stay. A proper rough couple were occupying the room next to me and they made their presence felt throughout the house day and night. He was a ginger skinhead, in his late twenty's, well-built, a hardman with a twitchy and unpredictable nature. One minute he was laughing and smiling, and the next minute he was in a rage and telling you about the people he had "smashed" on the previous weekend. His girlfriend was a small and slim brunette, similar age to him and equally as vicious. She was the clever one in the relationship and she seemed to manage the skinhead, like a Pitbull on a lead. They were both jobless, hanging around all day, which made the other tenants nervous. Whether it was putting up with their noisy sex at regular intervals or facing the mountain of dirty pots and dishes that they would rudely leave all in the kitchen sink.

The ginger skinhead and a thuggish mate came back from the pub very drunk one night and they started to bang on my room door. I could hear them talking loudly about beating up the “Fucking Paddy”. I hoped that it that was just big talk, drunken bravado, thugs trying to impress each other. I was pretending to be asleep but I was listening very closely for movement and any attempt to open the door. I prepared myself to get to my feet quickly and fight, if necessary. The thugs continued to threaten me from outside the door for several minutes, but they made no move. I decided to call them out, telling them to come into the room if they had something to say. They made some more noise, but they didn’t come in, thankfully. Things went quiet and the danger passed temporarily. This was hardly the dream start to my new life in England. I had to find another place to stay.

“Psycho House 2”

I was introduced to a man who worked in the hotel with me. He was a landlord with a beautiful room to rent in his loft conversion. He was a very average working-class man, middle-aged, short, balding, bland, permanent grey overalls and polished black shoes. He was quiet, inarticulate and unremarkable, but he seemed harmless to me. I moved in just in time for my first Christmas away from Ireland. But it was going to be a clear case of out of the frying pan and into the fire. Before I agreed to take the room, I did not know or fully appreciate that my landlord had a girlfriend who lived with him. She was half his age, but twice his size and she had been to prison several times for violent behaviour. However, there was a further twist to this unpleasant situation. She met her current boyfriend, my new landlord, when she was in a relationship with his son. It seems that I was drawn to highly dysfunctional homes. It did not take long before it got ugly.

I came back late one night to discover the house surrounded by police cars. As I entered, there was blood all over the kitchen floor. My landlord had been stabbed multiple times by his girlfriend with a kitchen knife. The police were questioning her in one room and he was separated in another room, walking wounded, with a terrified look on his face. Apparently, she only attacked him because she loved him, and he was too scared to tell the truth, so he said it was an accident. He was properly fucked now. If he tried to remove her she would kill him. If he continued to live with her, she would also kill him. His son had gifted him a complete nightmare. I got out quickly after that incident and moved into a flat share with a decent guy who was a similar age to me. Finally, some normality and my life in England started to settled down.

"Domestic Bliss"

My hotel job soon became very limiting and I found work in security again, which seemed to be a natural choice for me. Enthusiasm and hard work developed my security career quickly over the next few years. Pretty soon, I was wearing a shirt and tie, driving a company car and sporting a conspicuous 90's business pager to show that I was moving up in the world. I started to see a girl next door type from a conservative and middle-class family. Following a quick transformation, I was suddenly seeking a quaint little house with an orderly front garden in an English village. We moved our relationship forward way too fast, it was not organic and it was bound to fail. Before I knew it, wc had bought a home and I was staring into the abyss of oven-ready meals and watching boring TV every night. What the fuck was going on?

This period of my life was also the start of some very obvious mental struggles. I woke up agitated and I went to bed depressed, every day started to become painful for me. I was becoming two very different people simultaneously. One person was smiling politely at middle-class family dinners, discussing mortgages, interest rates and home furnishing. The other person was screaming on the inside, rebelling at work, highly prone to emotional outbursts, cheating, lying and avoiding responsibility. This double life was tearing me apart and the cracks in our relationship appeared very fast.

One summer evening, I was mowing the lawn after work, carefully cutting the neat and bordered grass edges to make sure it looked perfect. I stopped for a second and saw myself from a distance. I was imprisoned in a self-made cage and I knew that I had to end the relationship immediately. When my middle-class girlfriend came home later that evening, I sat her down and told her that I was not ready for commitment and our short relationship would have to end. Once I got that out, she took it pretty well and I think she was relieved deep inside. We agreed that she would move back in with her parents and I would stay in the house until it was sold. Domestic bliss was now officially over.

"Missing Daddy"

My early years living in England were unstable, I was so lost, trying unsuccessfully to find my feet and something to cling to. Inevitably, I started to reach towards a relationship and connection that I believed gave me safety. I wrote an emotional letter to Daddy to get our father and dutiful son show back on the road. I articulated my feelings over many pages and I was hoping that I could get a response from him. Mammy was at home when the letter arrived, she later told me that he opened it, had a glance at the first few lines, and then discarded it as a useless object without comment. Mammy was on hand and she immediately grabbed the letter, and it remained secure in her handbag over the years, along with the letters that I wrote to her. She was always very sentimental about such things. I was completely blinkered and stupid to believe that Daddy would read my letter and feel something resembling love.

Mammy did not like the silence between Daddy and me. She helped to initiate communication when the telephone was installed in our home in Ireland. This looked like progress, but there was a twist. Daddy glued the twelve push-down buttons normally used to dial out, they were stuck, so the phone could only accept incoming calls. He was particularly pleased with this miserable innovation. However, on the upside, I was able to call Mammy more freely. The conversation always started with Mammy, but pretty soon she would deliberately hand the phone to Daddy to force him to talk to me. This was uncomfortable initially and Daddy made me feel guilty about running away. But I did not fight back because I wanted to make peace for Mammy, and a big part of me missed the tyrant.

Soon there was regular communication between Daddy and me, and I was making plans to please him again. I took time off work and arranged for him to visit me in England. These trips were always suggested and managed by me, I can see now that he was not bothered. But I had some utility, Daddy could use the trips to see his two brothers and sister who lived in London at that time. I chauffeured him around and took care of all his needs and whims for a few days. In return, he might pay for a meal to let me know that I was lucky to have him around. Whilst in his company, I had to endure his constant complaining about my siblings. I had forgotten about how negative and vicious he was, but I didn't defend my family or challenge him. His authority and influence were firmly back in my life.

9. Drinking & Fighting

My career in security provided opportunities to work as a bouncer in clubs and bars. This extra income was useful, but there was also some motivation to pretend to the world that I was a hard man. To make the right impression, I joined a gym to build up my body and subsequently, the gym life became part of my identity and ego. The gyms that I frequented were full of monstrous men, with big muscles, big talk, flash cars and criminal lifestyles. They were so extreme, unpredictable and dangerous. These gangsters believed that they were invincible, but it was all borrowed and temporary power. Their flames burned out very quickly and violently in many cases. I was never really comfortable around those men, I was an outsider, trying to fit into another world.

"Gym Partner"

I was lucky enough to initiate a relationship with a really nice guy. My Gym Partner was Welsh, similar age to me, short and stocky, with blonde hair and almost transparent ice-white skin. He had a well-paid job in IT but he was not that flashy. He was shy but he had a steely calmness and a clear sense of himself. Knowing what I know now, I believe he was gay, but he hid it very well at the time. There were lots of tell-tale signs, secrecy about his love life, a pierced belly button, away every weekend but never sharing what he did. When I pointed out girls in the gym that I thought were attractive, he seemed to have a delayed reaction and just agreed with whatever I said.

We trained together five times a week and we made noticeable progress. But we were still much smaller compared to some of the gym monsters around us. We decided to try a course of steroids. I was curious about how it would work and the potential results. I knew a guy who was deep in the steroid business, both taking it and selling it and we set up a transaction. We met him on a side street one night and completed a cash-in-hand deal from the boot of his car. Small pharmaceutical packages with foreign language were passed over discreetly. Each box contained multiple vials of synthetic testosterone and deca-durabolin. I did not think about whether the steroids were safe or how they were going to affect me.

My Gym Partner came around to my place to inject the steroids for the first time. It was a very tense situation, the needles had to be very large for the viscous steroid liquid to pass through. My gym partner injected the steroids into the upper part of my ass cheeks, gluteus maximus, to be precise. He administered two injections, one of each type of steroid, and then it was my turn to inject him with the same dose. It was nerve-racking, we were sweating about where exactly to make the injection and how to dispose of the used needles safely. How funny this is now, pulling my pants down and bending over for my Gym Partner, knowing that he was probably gay. But he was always a very respectful man and never did anything to make me feel uncomfortable. We repeated this injection ceremony twice a week, and we planned to complete the full course over eight weeks.

The steroids had only a positive effect on my Gym Partner, he had muscle gain with no behaviour changes. However, I was a different case, things got out of shape very quickly. My sex drive went nuts as a starting point, suddenly every ex-girlfriend was looking much more attractive to me. Some of these girls had genuine feelings for me, but my hormonal urges and my lack of sensitivity stopped me from seeing the hurt that I was causing. I was picking them up and putting them down when I needed sex, they all deserved better. My body responded to the steroids very quickly and noticeably, I took a very average dosage but the results were huge. It took a couple of weeks to kick in, but once it did, I felt and looked very different. My chest and shoulders expanded, my legs exploded and my stance was more pronounced and powerful.

Taking steroids also has other effects, I was much more alert, focused and ready for action at all times. My aggression was progressively building and there were many problems and confrontational incidents. On one occasion, I stopped my car at the traffic lights to fight with some guys in the car behind me for simply beeping their horn. They drove off scared when I jumped out and violently banged on their car window with my fist. In my steroid rage, I wanted them all to get out and fight me. I was also reacting with excessive aggression in normal day-to-day situations, I pinned a work colleague to the wall for saying something virtually harmless to me. I grabbed him by the throat, lifted him clean all off the ground and held him there so that he would be in fear for his life. This was not me, this was a maniac, another person had taken control of me. I now understand what people describe as the "red mist", when they can only see violence as an option.

An Australian man joined our gym and it was clear from the first day he walked in that he wanted to mark his territory. He was a bull of a man, a square head like a concrete block, tall and thick, with hands that resembled two bunches of bananas. He was pushing his weight around the gym and he thought that I was a suitable target to dominate. I looked younger, smaller and isolated to him, but I had friends in that gym and I wanted to show people that I was able to take on a challenge. The

Australian man deliberately gave me some verbal abuse one day whilst I was training. He said that I had taken his weights, which is poor gym etiquette. We exchanged some words, but neither of us was ready to fight yet, it was just the initial primate sizing-up ritual. There was a palpable tension every time we were both in the gym, everyone knew that something was going to kick off.

The Australian man was in the gym on a Saturday afternoon, ignoring me superficially, but it was uncomfortable and I couldn't relax. Fighting in a gym is dangerous, many heavy objects could be easily grabbed and used. I needed to plan the right time to strike. I waited until he had strapped himself onto a bar that he was about to lift. Whilst he was kneeling with his hands and arms immobilised by the straps, I approached from behind and kicked him in the face without a warning. He fell to the ground, slumped over the bar and weights, he was unconscious. I inflicted some more blows to the body, but not to his head, I was nervous about the damage I had done already. The guys in the gym pulled me off him and helped the Australian man regain consciousness. He slowly got to his feet, looked at me, and then he realised the dirty move I had made on him. At least two front teeth were broken from the kick to the face he received from my right boot.

I had bitten off more than I could chew, but I owed him a fair fight. We went outside with the rest of the gym following as the audience. There was a stand-off for a bit, I was trying to avoid the inevitable, but eventually, we squared off and got ready to exchange blows. He threw wild swinging and looping punches that completely missed me, thank fuck. If one had connected, my head would have been taken clean off my shoulders. The fight quickly went to the ground, we wrestled and got stuck in a stalemate. Neither of us could establish a position of dominance or control to finish the fight. We both became exhausted and we agreed to stop and call it a day. The Australian man wanted to shake hands, but I knew it was not settled right. I had no bruises to match his damaged front teeth. This fight was far from over.

I didn't like training in that gym after that, I was always looking over my shoulder, waiting to be hit by something hard and heavy. I was also growing tired of the aggression and bullshit that came with those kinds of gyms. I can remember the specific moment I realised that

I wanted to change. I was halfway through my training session on my own and I heard a voice inside me saying "I am not enjoying this". I just put the weights down, walked straight out of that gym and switched to a new gym with no hard men or gangster types. I also realised that steroids were pushing me in the wrong direction, and I did not go back for further hormone enhancements. Unfortunately, I lost contact with my Gym Partner. I started to tease him about being gay, and he suddenly disappeared and made no further contact with me. I should have been a better friend.

"Drinking Partner"

During my first few years in England, I managed to avoid regular alcohol consumption, the gym life kept that behaviour at bay. However, at the age of twenty-five, I suddenly dived into a world of heavy drinking. The night that I met my Drinking Partner set the scene for our future relationship. We were both at a house party in the early hours of the morning. Everyone was sitting down on sofas in a large room, drunk and chilling out. Some people were smoking marijuana and having nice chats. It was summertime, a calm warm night and I had an idea to play to the crowd and get some attention. I left the room, removed all my clothes except my underwear and used a very large towel to create a superhero cape. I came back into the room and jumped up on the back of the sofa to gain elevation before delivering my theatrical lines. "Look in awe as the caped avenger flashes his crimson cape in the wind". It was so ridiculous, but it got the big laugh that I craved. I was out there, sticking out proudly, delighted with my stupidity. My relationship with my Drinking Partner started in that moment. We both connected to the same self-destructive tendencies and we both got a buzz from being the biggest clown.

My Drinking Partner was tall, athletic, stylish, well-travelled, university-educated, creative, with sophisticated taste in music. He was my age, but he knew much more about the world than me. However, once we started drinking together, the brotherly bond of competition, pushing boundaries and risk-taking commenced. I suspect our real connection was probably something that we did not acknowledge, we were both sensitive and confused boys. Rapid consumption of a litre of vodka was always our starting point before going out, to get us in the mood. Followed by endless shots at various bars and clubs to keep us going all night. To those looking on, we were a pair of louts looking for attention, but there was a sadness within both of us. After the alcohol had worn off, we would often find ourselves in profound conversations about our frustrations and unhappiness. It was at this time that family history and how it hurt us both came to the surface. But once Friday night arrived, all of that went away for a while and the heavy drinking show was back on the road.

"Instant Sex"

Going out with the boys, getting drunk, getting laughs, getting girls, this became a new high for me. My focus on girls was constant and everywhere, bars, clubs, gyms, supermarkets, walking down the street. Any place where I could sense any remote interest in me was an opportunity. I was always tuned in and ready to pounce. I had so many temporary girls coming in and out of my life, it was ridiculous. I was having sex with two or three different girls every week. They all eventually worked out I was playing the field, but I didn't feel the consequence. I simply moved on to the next target without a thought. Looking back now, I can see that I could not enjoy relationships. I was scared of intimacy and love. Bouncing from girl to girl helped me to avoid that fear, but it confused and hurt a lot of nice girls along the way. I wish that I had been more honest with them, and myself.

My first "boys' holiday" experience in a hot and foreign land was Greece in 2001. My Drinking Partner, a couple of friends and me were a gang of four young men with a simple mission. Drink endless vodka and fuck as many girls as possible. I thought that seven nights of pure fun awaited, but the actual outcome was surprising. We started on the first night of the holiday as we intended to go on, heavy drinking and bad behaviour. I was acting like a chimpanzee, shouting in restaurants, play fighting in the streets and humiliating innocent strangers passing by to entertain and seek attention. Being an obnoxious cunt was my task, and I excelled. I displayed my sexual confidence and I was with a different girl almost every night of that holiday. Some of them might have seen a flash of something good in me. But my behaviour quickly pushed them away and made them understand that I was not suitable boyfriend material.

Towards the end of the holiday and after repetitive nights of heavy drinking, I started to notice something unexpected creep into my consciousness. When I was in my most exhausted state, I started to hear an inner voice making noise in my head. Despite the drinks, laughs and action with the girls, I was unable to feel happy and satisfied. I was sobering up very fast and finding myself feeling lonely and depressed. I came back from that holiday very unsettled and I was questioning everything in my life. Something deeper was upsetting me but I could not grasp or articulate what it was. Part of me wanted to stop for a while, to work out what was wrong. However, most of me was still locked into a repetitive pattern of using alcohol and sex to keep me occupied.

My Drinking Partner was getting frustrated with our Saturday night hero lifestyle and the boring English commuter town that we lived in. He was also getting frustrated from hanging around with me. He could see my mental health problems and the addictive side of my nature manifesting itself. He warned me, but I did not listen to him. He was thinking big and he wanted to go travelling around the world to broaden his horizons. It was better for both of us that we parted ways at that time, I was not grown up enough to handle a trip around the world. When he left I was happy for him, I knew he had more to give, but I also felt a loss and perhaps even being abandoned. He had decided to grow up and I was left behind and stuck in my juvenile world.

"Messy Fights"

One of the consequences of heavy drinking for me was getting into fights. In a single week, I can remember being thrown out of three different bars for violent exchanges. I was in a terrible club one night and I managed to get myself into an unnecessary dancefloor confrontation with a group of frisky, tight-shirted young men. Before I knew it, I was being carried out in a stranglehold by five large bouncers. One of them was holding me by the neck and choking me, and the other four had a limb each. They carried me out of that club at shoulder height and clean off the ground. When they approached the exit to eject me, their final move was to throw me through the double doors. This let me know that I was not welcome back, in a very non-subtle way.

An Irish friend and me were having a kebab in town before going home very late on a Saturday night. There were crowds of noisy people leaving the busy bars spilling onto the streets. Groups of drunken guys were chatting and jostling excitedly, and pretty girls in high heels linked arms as they walked towards queues of taxis. This was a typical scene in most English towns every weekend. A tough-looking skinhead flanked by two trashy women approached us and gave me a dirty look as he walked past, he was sneering at me for some reason. I said “What are you looking at?” in my thick Irish accent. He then proceeded to call me a “Fucking Paddy” in a dismissive tone. The trashy women with him laughed at me as they walked off. The skinhead thought I was scared of him, but my Irish friend and I decided to go after him.

We followed him to the train station and my Irish friend immediately challenged the skinhead to a fight. They started to argue, but neither man made a move. The trashy women were not helping, they were getting involved and agitating the situation. I was standing back a few feet observing, but the confrontation was becoming pointless. I said to my Irish friend, "Let's go home", which made the skinhead switch his focus back to me and retort, "Who the fuck asked you?". Without warning, I stepped up to him and delivered a single rapid punch to the side of his head with my right arm. The skinhead fell down to the ground and was unable to get back to his feet. The trashy women had to pull him up and help him into a taxi located close by. As the taxi drove away, I could see the blood rushing down the side of his face from the cut I had opened on his head. This sudden violence took me by surprise. There was anger and frustration bending me out of shape.

"Lost & Depressed"

All of my twenties was a very unsettled period, I moved around a lot, buying and selling several properties. Each sale provided me with large sums of cash as the property market grew. However, I had very slippery hands when it came to managing money and I spent that cash quicker than setting fire to it. I went through a repetitive spending cycle, buy something, want to change it, throw it away and then start all over again. I was also taking on new credit without understanding the long-term impact, desperately signing myself up for any high-interest loan that allowed me to spend more. Expressing myself through material possessions took centre stage and I was building a mountain of crippling debt. I created signature man pads in each new town that I moved to, where nobody knew me or gave a fuck about me. If I stopped for a moment, I would have to face the past and myself, and I wanted to avoid this at all costs.

My career in security was going well and I found out to my own surprise, I was able to hold my own in the corporate world. I had a directness and drive for productivity that was useful in that world and I was appointed head of the department in a large organisation. Some of my work peers did not expect me or want me to achieve such a promotion, because I was arrogant and brash at times. Some of them even went out of their way to make me their enemy. I wasted time and energy pursuing conflict with these small and pointless people, I always had something to prove. Deep down, I didn't feel that I deserved the promotion and I couldn't enjoy it fully. I had reached a career position that I was not ready for. Everything in my life was accelerating, a bigger job, more responsibility, more cash, more debt. I could not manage all of these things, they possessed me and I was taken for a ride.

Despite the new job and the latest man pad project, the feeling of loneliness and depression would not go away. During this time, I became very drawn to moving and emotional music, songs about loss and tragedy. Some of the better works of Freddie Mercury and George Michael were on repeat play. There was something in the words and emotions of those songs that triggered subconscious pain and deeper feelings that I was trying to hold down. Whilst I was driving and listening to music, I would suddenly burst into tears unexpectedly and cry so hard that I would have to stop the car. I was just overwhelmed by it all, the music was upsetting me, but I did not understand why.

It started to become difficult to get out of bed in the morning, I felt heavy and troubled. There was a bleakness in my world that I just couldn't move. Dark thoughts and motivations began to intrude, my life seemed to be pointless and worthless, I felt that I was destined for tragedy. I took a big step and went to see a doctor, not a psychologist or a therapist, just the local general practitioner. We had a short surface chat and he was sympathetic, but he did not help me or point me in the right direction. We discussed anti-depressant medication, but something was telling me not to do it. Inevitably, I brushed my feelings under the carpet, hoping that it would go away. I needed help to break down the walls within me, and the source of this help came from a very unexpected place.

10. Clubs & Drugs

Top of the Pops was on TV every week through the 1980s and it influenced a generation. I can remember trying to discreetly watch it as a child, but if Daddy was home, he would immediately turn the TV off and sneer. Popstars and musicians were “junkies” and “devil worshippers” according to him. I tried to follow his rules, but part of me was always secretly affected by music. I used to hide in our front room sometimes and listen to the Rebel’s Whitney Houston tape cassette. The front room was the neutral ground, an isolated and cold place. A place where everyone went to avoid Daddy, whilst he sat holding power in the kitchen. The emotional ballads really affected me and I used to sing and dance awkwardly to the music when there was nobody around. There was always a deep connection to music within me, waiting to ignite.

"Vauxhall Part 3"

Vauxhall became a magnetic place for me during times of important change. I was there in 1991 during my first solo trip to London as a sixteen-year-old. I landed there again in 1994 on a Friday night after I ran away from home. Through the twists and turns of life, Vauxhall featured once again in 2004 when I was twenty-nine years old at the start of a new journey. There were many underground clubs in Vauxhall at this time. Straight, gay, mixed and hardcore clubs open to everyone, take your pick. All concealed in the dark recesses of the bricked railway arches running through the centre of Vauxhall, a busy junction of roads, rail and river. These clubs started on a Thursday night and finished on a Monday morning. Partying was available through the weekend if you wanted it. Conspicuous drug dealers were located in convenient and accessible locations throughout the clubs, to aid the quick flow of dirty cash notes in exchange for whatever drugs you needed. It was straightforward supply and demand.

"Welcome to Fire"

There was one particular Vauxhall club that stood out through this time. The first time that I went to Fire was a Friday night. There was a very long queue and I eventually got through the doors at around 2 am. As I walked into the main room, the energy on the dance floor almost lifted me off my feet. The music was visceral and went right through my body. There seemed to be no rules in this club, wear what you want and do what you want. There were well dressed rich people sniffing cocaine in the toilets, hairy gay men kissing in dark corridors, wide-eyed ravers stomping on the dancefloor and strippers relaxing after work. It was a wild and chaotic jungle, but it always felt safe to me. Everyone was welcome and I was instantly and completely intoxicated by Fire.

During the early stages of my Fire era, I found myself alone in the club at around 5 am. Being on my own was fine, I often preferred it that way. I was sitting on a sofa in a dark corner of the club, kicking back and feeling the music, I was warm, relaxed and surrendered.

Feel good serotonin induced by ecstasy was swooshing through my body and my worries lifted away for a while. A voice from somewhere inside of me started to tell me that I was not the hard person that I was pretending to be, I was sensitive and I needed love. Maybe I was not the angry and closed person that Daddy created. There were some tears as I sat still and let my feeling wash over me. It was not sadness, it was relief and the start of a necessary breakthrough.

A crucial part of the club experience is dancing. Not the type of polite and self-conscious dancing you might see at a wedding or a boring party. I am talking about drug-fuelled and uninhibited dancing that takes over your body and compels you to jump and move in a way that makes you feel pure joy. I never really had the urge to dance when I was drinking alcohol, I am not a particularly good dancer and my dancefloor activity was usually focused on meeting girls. However, the effect of ecstasy, the music and the electric atmosphere in Fire got me to my feet and onto the dancefloor to move and express myself. Feelings and emotions that were locked inside suddenly erupted. I was dancing on my own, bouncing in all directions, bare-chested and letting go.

Every Friday night was peak excitement for me when 10 pm approached and Fire was ready to open. I would drive as fast as possible to get to Vauxhall, speeding through London traffic to the sound of pumping music. Park on a side street close by and run the short distance into the club to get things started. Once I was in the door and I had secured a supply of ecstasy, I was at home and feeling good. A weekend of action and escapism lay ahead and that was all I could think about. It did not take long before I developed a reputation in Fire as a regular face. I arrived when the club was barely open and I never knew when it was time to go home.

Fire was a mixed gay club, and this was a big advantage for me. There was hardly any competition from testosterone-fuelled straight men. I got plenty of attention from girls in the club and I had too many sexual encounters to count. One night, I was chatting to a sexy Brazilian girl on the dancefloor, but I was high and the music was so loud that I could not hear her properly. We were chatting for several minutes and everything seemed to be going well. I then realised that she had been trying to tell me that she had stayed in my flat recently and we had sex. Even after she told me this fact, and I stopped to have a proper look at her face, I still struggled to place her. She told me that I had given her some tracksuit bottoms the following morning to travel home because her little dress was ripped. I was wondering for days where those blue Adidas bottoms went. The mystery was finally solved.

Friday, Saturday and Sunday nights in Vauxhall clubs blended into one, and it completely consumed my life for a few years. My weekends were full of exploration and highs but the early part of the next week was a bleak comedown. The cold reality of Monday floored me as I tried to get back to my conventional life. Driving to work in the morning became a new experience, staring at the world in a state of confusion.

The natural green of the trees along the road was suddenly so strong and vivid. I could see animated nature fighting back against the grey and cold man-made buildings. The conventional things that I previously believed were certain and fixed now appeared to be silly and temporary. These experiences were re-wiring my head. It was an awakening but it was overwhelming at times. I found myself crying almost every day, as I struggled to accept a new reality.

"Clubbing Partner"

It's hard to judge character accurately when you are in a club, high and searching for adventure in the dark. I made some friends in those wild times, we all changed along the way but the genuine connections have stood the test of time. My Clubbing Partner and I met in the summer of 2005, and we immediately became partners in crime. He was born and bred in London, five years younger than me, good-looking, gay, musical, a performer and a very kind soul. He came from a very humble and challenging start, but he gets on with life, despite the cards that he was dealt. We never really discussed the specifics of the dysfunctional families that we were both running away from. But it is clear to me that this shared experience of trauma has connected us from the start.

It was Christmas Eve and we were hanging around in Fire, it was the obvious place to be. We were chatting and it was clear from our conversation that my Clubbing Partner was not looking forward to his family Christmas dinner. He wanted to avoid this gathering for many reasons, but one of the reasons was that he knew that his cousin would be there. His cousin was the same age as him, born in the same hospital and almost on the same day, but he had taken a very different road as a young man. Their lifestyles clashed and I sensed from the conversation that there was some tension troubling my friend. So, we stayed in Fire as long as possible and my friend avoided the family Christmas dinner. This turned out to be an important missed opportunity.

"Miami"

In early January, I received a shocking call from my Clubbing Partner. The cousin that he avoided on Christmas day had been murdered. It was very tragic and

I wanted to help my friend in any way that I could. Some of the affected family were based in Miami and my friend needed to travel there. I volunteered to join him and provide support in the aftermath. He needed to be with family, but he also wanted to have a few days with me to take his mind off things. I had never been to America at this stage and I was also looking forward to seeing some of places you see in the movies. However, my trip to Miami was going to be extraordinary in a way I could not have anticipated.

We shared a double hotel room in South Beach and we went out to relax on the first night, it was a Thursday. Initially, we did not discuss his murdered cousin, we avoided the subject, but it was definitely hanging around somewhere in the background. The first night was full of bars and heavy drinking, it was a total wild blur and we got separated in the madness. True to form, I ended up having sex with some random girl in an outdoor pool as the residents watched on from their balconies. I sloped back to our hotel in the morning to meet up with my Clubbing Partner, he also had a naughty adventure to share. Miami is such a cool place, but Miami is also a dangerous place. A few wrong steps in the wrong direction can put you in a place where you could be in serious trouble. Despite the reputation, I felt safe there for some reason.

We went out again on Friday night to a club called "Nocturnal". It looked like a popular place when we joined the long queue. The camp club host was moving up and down the street and eyeing up the would-be customers. He stopped to examine us and have a little chat, assessing our potential. My Clubbing Partner and I had the distinct advantage of English and Irish accents respectively and a different fashion sense compared to the local crowd. We were directed to go straight in without paying the fee, we felt like superstars. The warm night, the pumping music, the drinks, the glamorous people, it was an amazing club. Added to this infectious party atmosphere, cocaine was freely available and very pure. Processed crystals from the South American coca leaf had my dopamine receptors firing on all cylinders. I enjoyed the cocaine, but it was not centre stage yet, ecstasy was still my preferred option.

We got separated again that night and met back at the hotel in the morning. Saturday was spent recovering, our bodies were officially unresponsive. We watched Miss America on TV that night in our little Miami world. I think I picked Miss Texas to win and my Clubbing Partner picked some other Barbie doll, and we laughed and we distracted ourselves for a few hours. We continued to avoid any discussion about his murdered cousin, but his presence was not far away. Following a decent sleep, we woke up early on Sunday morning and went to Miami Space to enjoy the daytime club experience in the sunshine. Once again, our distinct accents and out-of-town looks were noticed by the club host in the long queue and we were sent straight in the door without paying any fee. We were on a natural high as we rushed through the doors, eager to see what was happening inside. We looked at each other and without saying a word, we both knew that it was going to be a wild one.

Miami Space was an aesthetic club, plastic surgery for the girls and steroids for the boys. It was glamorous and cool, but still not trying too hard. We made some new party friends instantly and pretty soon we were receiving multiple invites to after-parties. We were being enticed with exciting offers of what lay in wait, pools, drugs and famous people. When we said we had already accepted an invite to a different party, our would-be hosts dismissed the other invitations and sold their offer even harder. America is truly about sell, sell, sell. Our foreign accents were seen as interesting and everyone wanted to display us at their party as exotic trophies to entertain.

"Adults Only"

We danced and revelled in our role as social butterflies. By late afternoon, we had left Space and we were heading towards an unknown location in a car with some party people. We had no idea who they were or what kind of party we were going to. We arrived at a big modern house in a private and upmarket residential area. An attractive and virtually naked blonde woman in her 30s with huge breast implants answered the front door and ushered us in. We walked through the luxurious house, into a vast marbled kitchen and then outside to the garden and pool area located at the back. There were about 20 people at the party, all wearing poolside clothing or swimwear. The first thing that I saw was a very large bald man who looked like he should be a WWE wrestler and he was eating the naked ass of an accommodating woman. She was lying on a sun lounger, face down, with her ass perched stiffly in the air. He was kneeling and eating away from behind, nobody batted an eyelid, apparently very normal at this kind of party.

My Clubbing Partner and I held our reactions inside, we did not want to appear inexperienced or shocked. Our hosts provided us with swimming shorts, and we jumped into the pool and moved to a quiet spot to discuss our game plan discreetly. This house was miles from anywhere, we were brought there by strangers and we had no easy way back to the hotel. Our plan was "Let's stick together and see how this goes". Various party people showed up and then left as the day progressed and we had to explain our accents several times over, amid the ass-eating and cocaine consumption. We had a front-row ticket, it all seemed glamorous and hedonistic, but things are not always what they seem. I could sense tension due to various sexual pursuits and partner swapping activity. People at these parties always pretend that they are free spirits and there is no jealousy, but that is rarely true. My Clubbing Partner and I hooked up with some romantic interests as the party faded and we headed off in different directions once again.

"Hotel Visit"

I headed back to the hotel in South Beach on Monday morning, expecting to find my Clubbing Partner recovering in bed. However, for some strange reason, when I arrived at our hotel room door, I opened the door cautiously and I did not proceed inside. Something made me wait there before entering. From the doorway, I could see down the long hallway that led to the main part of room, but I could not see the lounge and the beds. You had to walk down the hallway and turn to the left to reveal the main part of the room. I stood in the doorway and I called out to him "Are you alone?". He responded in an alert and definite voice that said "yes", but he said no more than that. I could not see him, but I sensed that there was someone else there with him. I waited in the doorway and I asked him again, "Are you sure you are on your own?", he said "yes" once again, and then remained silent. I was not satisfied with his answer.

I walked down the hallway very slowly and I entered the main room. My friend was lying in bed, body facing down, his head positioned to the side looking in my direction. He was frozen still with the bed covers pulled right up to his neck. I walked around the room, the situation was suspicious, but my friend did not move, only his eyes followed me. I still sensed that someone else was there and I just didn't believe him. He became more anxious as I started to examine a specific corner in the main room, there was energy drawing me there. He then whispered to me that he had been trapped in bed for hours, watching, whilst the spirit of his murdered cousin was walking up and down in the corner of the room that I had been drawn to. I sat down on the bed and comforted my friend. We both felt the visitor and it was now time to talk properly about his loss and grief. Perhaps his cousin was trying to say goodbye because he was taken without warning. I hope that he has found peace somewhere.

“Ibiza”

I went to Ibiza with an Irish friend, but we had very different agendas from the start. I wanted to eat the whole island, but my Irish friend was seeking a chilled-out break with some sun. He was not a heavy drinker and he always said no to drugs. We arrived on a Thursday afternoon and immediately hit the beach. I found drugs in a busy bar and started as I meant to go on. An English party girl from up north was flirting with me and looking for action. She was in her late twenty’s, tall, fit, with black hair pulled back off her face and tied up in a ponytail, wearing a mini skirt, bikini bra and boots. Her primary marketing strategy was her enormous breast implants that could be seen from a considerable distance. I often went for girls like this back then.

Later that night, I met her again in Club Penelope. Drinks, pumping music, ecstasy and dancing were enjoyed, and I went back to a cheap hotel with the party girl. It is hard to know what sex will be like with a stranger, especially when drugs are involved, but this one was very unexpected. She kept talking to me about how incest was a sexual turn-on, and she repeatedly shouted "Do you want to fuck your sister?!" whilst we were in the act. It was weird and it was a little distracting, who knows how she got to such a fucked-up place. I got out of there very quickly in the morning after an awkward goodbye, and avoided her for the rest of the holiday.

My Irish friend and I went back to Club Penelope again on Friday and Saturday night, but I was starting to stray away from him. We parted ways and I did not see him for a couple of days. I think he was happy to opt out and relax, he already had enough of watching me get high as a kite. Ibiza is a friendly place and there is a consensus that everyone should have a good time whilst on the island. I often found myself alone in clubs and it did not bother me. There was a certain risk and excitement that comes with going solo and finding your way in the chaos. I connected with some party people in Club Penelope, a group of around six, similar age to me and of mixed nationality, Brazilian, Dutch, and Spanish. As Saturday night progressed to Sunday morning, we headed to Ibiza Space to catch the sunrise on the iconic Space terrace.

"Zombie Driver"

We gathered outside the club to organise transport, but we needed more than one taxi to carry everyone to Space. Myself and a Brazilian guy in the party group got separated. Before I could say no, we ended up in a bashed up Fiat Punto with some random Italian guys who offered us a lift to Space. We just jumped in enthusiastically, only to find that the driver was so high that he could hardly see in front of himself. I am not certain what combination of drugs the driver was on. I suspect Ketamine, which is a tranquiliser and not helpful for driving, and something else to straighten him up, cocaine or speed is possible. He was fucking out of it. Slurring badly in an Italian accent and steering all over the road whilst looking behind himself and driving forward at speed. The sun was coming up, so at least there was some daylight to guide the zombie driver. I was sitting in the back seat with the Brazilian guy and we gave each other that look of knowing. No words were needed, we both knew we would just have to hold on and hope for the best.

I was ready to jump in the front seat and grab the steering wheel or potentially stop the car, but only as a last resort because that could cause the car to crash. The journey seemed to go on forever, the fucked-up driver was obviously lost. After a tense few minutes with everyone trying frantically to direct the driver, miraculously, the little Fiat Punto came to a stop close to Space. Myself and the Brazilian guy jumped out of the car as quickly as possible, feeling lucky that we had survived this ride of terror. We got into Space just in time to catch the sunrise from the terrace. It was beautiful, just like everyone who has experienced it tells you.

Ibiza Space during the daylight was a very pleasant place to be. Hordes of open-minded and attractive people coming together to share something special. Uplifting music, dancing in the summer sun, drinks, drugs, muscular boys with their tops off and pretty girls in bikinis, everyone getting carried away in a hedonistic moment. I spent the whole day in Space and I was the life and soul of the party. Passers-by were the victims of my dramatic physical jokes, picking people up on the dancefloor and holding them over my head. This gave me the other drug that I craved, attention. As the afternoon progressed into the evening at Space, the sun and the bright daylight disappeared and the party people that I met drifted away. I realised that I was on my own again, but I did not want to stop.

I needed a change of scenery. A quick visit to my hotel to get cleaned up and I was out again seeking adventure. Some party people that I met arranged a guest list for me at Club Privilege. I took a taxi there and flew in the door, passing many jealous faces in the queue. Privilege was a huge club with many things happening at the same time, designed to stimulate and overwhelm the euphoric crowds. Multiple themed rooms, computerised visuals, extravagant decoration, beautiful dancers and live sex shows. Everywhere you looked, something grabbed your attention and hijacked your senses. The club was so busy, thousands of people moving around like furious ants. I had been high for days, and my energy levels were starting to run low. Despite the drugs, I was walking now, not running.

The music in Privilege that night was different, less of a happy pumping dance beat, more dark vocals and mixes of moody sounds. I came to a stop and I was just watching people as they streamed past me in every direction. They all seemed so purposeful, but where were they going? Why was I there? What was I looking for? I then saw myself standing there isolated, silent, lonely and everybody was ignoring me. All of my sabotaged relationships, fuck ups, regrets, debts and everything that I was ashamed of hit me at once. I felt useless and completely lost, and I did not know how to put things right. I was sickened and I have never felt so alone in my entire life.

The music in the club started to reach inside of me, the DJ was mixing the Killer's song “Mr Brightside”. I could hear the lyrics so clearly, the words seemed to be talking directly to me, vibrating in my bones. The emotions in the song triggered something inside of me. I realised that I had thrown away the opportunity for love many times and now I was standing there all alone. I listened deeply as the song chorus repeated and the words told me what to do “But it’s just the price I pay, destiny is calling me, open up my eagle eyes”. There is no doubt that an exhausted state and chemical diet contributed to my twisted reality. But I knew that everything that was happening to me was just a sign and that I must try to move forward. I was upset, but the weight of loneliness lifted away and part of me knew that I was pushing myself to extremes to feel the necessary pain. If I listen to that song now it can take me back to that place instantly, and the words give me strength.

I left Privilege and Space seemed like the best place to go, it was familiar. More drugs were purchased on the way via the taxi driver, his stash was located down a deserted dark road in an old stone wall. If I was a different person, I would have marked the location and gone back there later. But that kind of danger is not my thing, I was always happy to pay for drugs. Once I arrived in Space, there were more drinks, emptying my bank account and reaching the limit of everything. I was knocking about with a small group of people I had seen several times during the weekend. We were all hoping that the party would never end. I stayed in Space until morning and into Monday afternoon. But the time to leave Ibiza was approaching fast and my flight back to England was later that evening.

My Irish friend was waiting back at the hotel, rested and relaxed. I must have appeared like a wild animal to him when I arrived back. My suitcase was packed in a crazy state and I booked out of the hotel. We tried to have dinner, but I couldn't eat because my mouth was too sore from days of taking drugs and no sleep. In desperation, I bought some sleeping tablets and took a mouthful as we jumped into a taxi to the airport. This was a risky thing to do, and by the time we arrived at the airport, I was struggling to get through check-in. I was almost unconscious just before boarding, but my Irish friend carried me onto the plane. He had to slap my face as he carried me down the aisle and helped me into my seat. I am lucky that he was there for me. There were probably plenty of onlookers staring and commenting on my state, but I was too out of it to see their looks of disapproval. It is hard to think that I was this bad.

11. Warning Signs

There were many incidents and warnings signs during those years of going out and being wild that were telling me to stop pushing my luck. But I ignored the obvious evidence available to me and continued taking risks. I admire the average person who can consume alcohol and drugs in a measured and regulated way to aid social enjoyment. Alcohol and drugs have always instantly changed my energy and behaviour and pushed me into reckless and dangerous situations. I used to tell myself that I was strong, in charge and switched on. This was a delusion. I was deliberately putting myself in danger over and over, searching for something.

"Close Shave 1"

It was the middle of the summer and the kind of warm and humid weather that encourages people to stay outside chatting until the early hours. I attended a posh club to pursue some silly girls with my Irish friend. Neither of us was successful that night, a Rolex and the keys to a Ferrari where required to charm the girls in that kind of place. Afterwards, we went back to his place and we talked for about an hour. It was an unexpected conversation, I said more than I wanted to. I was depressed, tearful and very frustrated with my life. We drank a lot of alcohol that night but somehow, I felt sober and I wanted to go home to my own bed. I decided to drive the 20-mile trip and I told myself that I would be fine. My Irish friend offered me his spare room, but I wanted to shut myself off and be alone.

I took the quieter country roads home, avoiding the main roads and the motorway, just in case I came across the police. I was almost all the way home, about two miles away, but I was bursting to urinate. The urge was so bad, that I decided to stop the car by the side of the road to achieve a quick release. I jumped out, left the engine running, lights on, driver door open, and I was in the middle of urinating when a police car pulled up beside me. There were two young police officers in the car, a male officer driving and a pretty blonde female officer in the passenger seat. The female officer leaned out of her open window and shouted “Oi, that’s not very nice”.

I should have parked the car and shut the engine off so that the police would not made the connection between my bladder pressure and my method of transport. It did not take a high-ranking detective to work out that I could have been drinking and driving. I immediately turned on the charm, explained to them that I had a long journey and that I was nearly home, and I apologised. The female officer had a long look at me and said "Don't do that again", and they drove off. I thought that I had a lucky escape and got back into my car and drove off slowly.

The police car was driving away and fading into the distance in my rear-view mirror. They were probably discussing my roadside stop and whether they should have investigated further. I started to relax, but when I looked in my rear-view mirror again, the police car had turned around and was accelerating after me with blue lights flashing. I thought about trying to lose them for a second, but I knew it would make the situation much worse. They pulled me over and they took my breath sample, I was over the alcohol limit and I was arrested. They handcuffed me and I was placed in the back of their car to be transported to the police station. It all happened so fast, I was in shock, it was surreal, but part of me knew that I had brought it on myself.

A very no-nonsense police officer booked me into the station. I stared at the serious faces stood behind the custody desk and the official surroundings, this was now becoming more like reality. The next stage of the process was for me to provide a further breath sample on the station alcohol testing machine. This would give an accurate digital reading of my alcohol level. I blew in the tube as instructed, and the results were printed instantly by the machine for examination. I was over the limit, but not excessively, I was within a certain legal tolerance that allowed me to ask for a blood sample for accuracy. This was my lucky break.

Whilst we waited for the doctor to administer the blood test, I was locked in a police cell. I remember it very well, a featureless white concrete square room, a steel toilet and a single hard bench to lay on. The cell had a large metal door that banged and locked shut with complete certainty. In many situations in my life, I could always run away or fight my way out. Those options were removed from me in that police cell. I remember the feeling of being trapped and defeated, it was a feeling that I never want to have again. There was shouting and aggressive noises coming from the other cells. It wouldn't stop, it seemed that the police were trying to control a violent prisoner. The doctor was delayed during this chaos and I sensed an opportunity.

I jumped to the floor and I began to do press-ups. When my shoulders and arms were too tired, I did a step-up exercise on the cell bench repetitively to work the muscles in my legs, then I switched back to press-ups when my legs were tired. I repeated my police cell training over and over, and I went as hard and as fast as I could. I knew that getting everything in my body going would reduce the alcohol in my blood. After about 30 minutes of non-stop and determined police cell training, the doctor finally arrived to take my blood. He used a needle to extract the sample and then packed it to be sent away to the relevant laboratory for analysis.

The police wanted to put me back in the cell until the morning, but I asked to have a go on the station alcohol testing machine again. I blew in the tube and we waited for the digital printed report to come out. The new breath sample was good, I was now under the legal limit and the police could not hold me in the station. The pretty blonde female officer who had arrested me at the roadside sensed that my blood sample may also be under the limit, as it was taken just a couple of minutes before. She was annoyed and she gave me a dirty look as she escorted me out to freedom.

I walked out of the police station into a bright Sunday morning. It was very early, the roads were quiet and there was nobody around to see my head hanging down low with shame. I took the long walk to pick up my car at the scene of the arrest. As I drove home, I was in shock and numb, realising that I may have caused some damage that I could not fix easily. It was impossible to sleep, so I lay down on the cold wooden floor in my flat with a single cushion under my head, staring up at the ceiling. I was consumed by frantic thoughts and trying to work out the meaning of this unexpected situation. I was doing the same shit every week, girls, drinking, drugs, driving recklessly, pushing, repeat, repeat. I just lay on the floor all day, thinking and hoping that I would be ok.

I decided to hide the incident from everyone until I knew the outcome. A few tense weeks passed by slowly before the blood sample results arrived. I was waiting for that specific letter, it would mean either an appearance in court and losing my driving licence, or maybe I would escape punishment. If I was convicted, I would lose my job. The letter was waiting for me on the floor inside my front door when I returned home from work one day. It was an official-looking brown envelope marked by the police. I opened it carefully and to my delight, luck was on my side once again. The results showed my alcohol was below the legal limit when the blood sample was taken by the doctor. No further action. My police cell workout had been effective.

"Close Shave 2"

The scene for another close shave ironically started in a Vauxhall club called “Crash”. I was hanging around with a cute girl from Australia and her gay housemate. The club was fun, but we decided to go back to their flat in East London to have a little party. I had taken some ecstasy pills that night but no alcohol, so I thought I was fine to drive. However, before we left, I decided to buy some extra drugs to entertain my hosts. The transaction was completed swiftly and I placed the gram of cocaine in the front right-hand pocket of my jeans. In my excitement to get out of the club and to the party, I didn’t conceal the drugs in my underwear. This oversight was going to be a problem.

We jumped into my Mini Cooper and started the journey to East London. Music was pumping, everyone was laughing and talking excitedly, it seemed like the perfect ending to a good night out. The roads were empty and I wanted to show how my Mini Cooper could take corners at high speed. We crossed the river Thames heading towards Westminster, accelerating over the bridge to the delight of my passengers. However, in my eagerness to impress, I did not notice that there was a police car behind me. Suddenly there was blue flashing lights in my rear view. I knew that I could not get away from the police in central London, they were well-prepared for such scenarios. My heart sank and I was pulled over very close to the House of Parliament. I needed to take control of the situation to survive this crisis.

Before the police could approach me, I got out of my car, shut the door and walked towards the two young officers casually. My instincts told me that it was better to leave my party friends inside the car, they would complicate matters. I immediately apologised for speeding and I said it was a new car and that I was still enjoying the novelty. They laughed and they said they wanted to chase me, they had not pursued a Mini Cooper yet. They thought that I would have a good chance of getting away from them on the empty city roads. I joked with the young officers, saying that they had pulled me over next to the House of Parliament to make me feel the full force of English law. They picked up on my Irish accent and we all laughed nervously, as we tried to get on with this awkward situation.

The police checked out the car, it was a company car, so it had all the right tax and insurance. Then they wanted to test my breath for alcohol, I said that was cool, knowing that I had not touched a drink that night. When they asked where I had been that night, I openly said I was out at a club but I was driving some friends home. Everything was going to plan, but then something unexpected happened. They had to call for a separate police van to bring the required alcohol test for some reason. It took maybe ten minutes for the van to arrive. During this waiting time, I was chatting furiously with the young officers to divert their attention, I must have appeared nervous. When the police van eventually arrived, my party friends were still trapped in my car and watching the scene unfold. They were unaware of the conversation and the sight of a police van arriving made them think that we were all going to the station for the night. I took the alcohol breath test, it was fine, but there was a final test before I would be allowed to go.

The young police officers started chatting with the officers in the police van about their next move. The officers in the van were older and wiser, and they told the young officers to give me a body search before releasing me. This was problematic, I still had a gram of cocaine in my front right-hand side pocket. Before the body search, one of the young officers said the standard police line "Do you have anything on your person that you shouldn't have?". My response to him was immediate and designed to distract. I said, "Only a gun in one pocket and a kilo of cocaine in the other", whilst pretending to search myself and patting down both of my front pockets. I held eye contact with the officer who intended to search me and the world stood still for a few seconds. The two young officers looked at each other, laughed and said goodnight. Another lucky escape.

"Close Shave 3"

Nights out and heavy drinking with the boys lost its appeal over time. I had moved on to dance clubs and ecstasy, and I did not enjoy the drunken and loutish antics like before. However, I stepped back in time and went out drinking with the boys in Brighton on a Saturday night. We went to a normal straight club, I had forgotten how silly these places were. Gangs of glossy girls being pursued by pumped-up boys. Inevitably, I got into a confrontation with some random angry guy in a tight shirt, I can't even remember what caused it. But I backed off before a full-scale fight commenced. This tense environment made me leave the club immediately without letting my friends know and make my way to Vauxhall on my own.

I reached Fire in the early hours of Sunday morning. My alcohol buzz was replaced with an ecstasy and I hit the dance floor. Fire was so different from the aggression I felt in Brighton earlier that night. I met many familiar faces and I felt warm and safe again. I stayed in Fire for several hours, right up to Sunday lunchtime, but I was getting tired now and I wanted to go home. In the daylight hours, it was easier to blend in as a normal driver, the police were generally not focused on stopping cars. I drove out of London and onto the motorway to complete the journey home. The route was very familiar to me and I was not expecting anything to go wrong.

My little Mini Cooper was fitting in nicely with the Sunday motorway traffic. But I was going too fast when I tried to take my exit and I spun around in the road. My car hit the metal barriers on one side of the road, and then violently bounced back across the road and ended up in the verge. Time seemed to stand still, it happened so fast but also so clearly. I can still recall the exact movements of the car as I lost control. Miraculously, the car did not flip over and I avoided a collision with the steady stream of cars hurtling past as they also left the motorway. My ears were ringing, but there were no broken bones and no blood. I appeared to have no physical injury, but the same good fortune could not be said for my Mini Cooper. The little car was crumpled, contorted and a complete write-off.

My ability to walk was tested first, after I slowly peeled myself out of the car and stood up. Legs and arms seemed to function satisfactorily. More practical tasks then came to mind, I had to get out of there before the police arrived. Passing cars stopped at the scene of the accident to see if I was ok and a nice Welsh family offered to help. I asked them to drop me home, my place was only two miles away and they kindly agreed. My car was on the side of the road, it was not obstructing traffic and I needed to make a quick escape to avoid the law. The Welsh family had just about enough space to accommodate me in their little car. We made polite small talk during the short journey and they did their best to help their unexpected passenger. They were genuinely good people and this drama probably gave them an interesting story to talk about for the rest of the day.

I called the police immediately when I arrived home, but before I could explain, they informed me that my crashed car had already been recovered. I had just missed them. They were annoyed that I had left the scene of an accident, but I said that my car was safe and that nobody was hurt. My strategy relied on the fact that the police would not be able to trace the car to my home address because it was registered with my employer. I allowed a couple of days to pass to let the dust settle before going to the police station. When they asked me why I left the scene of an accident, I said that I was in shock after the violent crash. The officer questioning me was suspicious, sniffing that something was not right, but he knew it was too late. Once again, I had narrowly avoided the serious consequences of my reckless behaviour.

12. The Witch

I was weaving through the dancefloor in Fire on a Friday night in December 2006. The place was packed with party people, flashing lights and pumping music coming at me from all directions. I turned a corner and accidently bumped into what seemed to be a very normal woman. She stood back from me, looked me up and down and she then just stared at me with an arrogant grin. She was daring me to speak to her. The challenge intrigued me, so I started a conversation, not knowing exactly what I was dealing with. She was Russian, about thirty years old, slim, pretty face, short black hair, very pale skin and completely black eyes. She was dressed expensively, a short purple velvet dress, designer jewellery and a large diamond-encrusted Chanel watch. Her confidence was mysterious and she was acting like she didn't care about anything in the world.

The Witch invited me to come back to her place after a short time chatting, she said she wanted to get out of the crowd. There was a woman with her in Fire that night, English, about forty, average looking with dirty blonde hair. I initially assumed that this woman was her friend, but she was from a different world and had a very specific role. The Witch sat in the front to give me directions, as we drove back to her place. The friend sat in the back seat, not joining in the conversation or giving away too much about herself. As we headed west through the city, the area and the properties were getting progressively more exclusive. We pulled up beside a very posh apartment building on the river, this was her place. The building had layers of security and staffed gates. This was a building designed to separate the rich from the poor and keep strangers out. We parked in an underground car park which was crammed with luxury sports cars owned by the residents. Then we walked through several security doors, used the lift, and eventually reached her apartment. The entire journey from building entry to her door was covered by CCTV.

Her apartment was huge, modern, with river views, but she was not the owner. It was rented for her by her "Russian boyfriend". A powerful man with homes all over the world and a girl in every city. As soon as we entered the apartment, she was straight on the phone to him, speaking in Russian and having a very loud and excited conversation. I should have left immediately, but my sense of danger was subdued by the drugs in my system. Adding to the complexity of the situation, the English woman with her was not her friend. She had a professional relationship with the Russian boyfriend, organising high-end sex parties for him and those who could afford to indulge in whatever they desired. She pretended to look after the Witch, going to parties with her, but she was spying for the Russian boyfriend. The Witch knew this was the case, but she played along with this dark and twisted game.

I stayed in the apartment for a while and we tried to have some fun, but the situation quickly became awkward. My better instincts kicked in and I made an excuse to go. The Witch took my phone number before I left, and to my surprise, she was keen to meet up. I was a little cautious for obvious reasons, the presence of a Russian boyfriend somewhere in the world unnerved me. Better not to run after her, so I sent her a text message to let her know where I would be over the weekend. I was standing in a club on the Saturday night with some friends, everyone relaxed and having a nice time. Suddenly, there was an intruder, the Witch appeared and pushed her way past everyone to get close to me. She then stood in my face, swaying drunk, high and very hostile. She did not introduce herself to my friends and she didn't care about how rude she was being. Her black eyes were firmly fixed on me.

I stayed in the Witch's luxury apartment that night and our dangerous relationship began. I saw her every weekend and sometimes during the week through December and into the new year. She had an endless supply of cash and cocaine and many doors opened for her. All the people around her that I met were vampires. Not a genuine smile or anything resembling honesty could be observed. The thing that made this even worse, the Witch knew that these people were vampires, but she enjoyed the game. She had been living like this for a long time, seeing people either fall at her feet or try to use her. There was also tension between me and the sleazy men who were creeping around her. They were threatened by me and the Witch enjoyed this conflict.

The Russian boyfriend was in touch by phone regularly, looming menacingly in the background. I put him out of my mind to avoid thinking about the potential consequences. The Witch pursued a loveless life, spending her days with cocaine as her best friend and hanging around sleazy vampires by night. I couldn't understand what she was doing. It was like she wanted to take everyone down to her version of hell. All my friends told me to keep away from her, but I ignored their concern and laughed it off. I thought I could deal with the risk, but this situation could get on top of me very easily. If I encountered her Russian boyfriend and his bodyguards whilst I was in her apartment, I was fucked. They would hurt me or maybe even worse if I fought back. I was rolling the dice every time I was with her.

The Witch hired an expensive private table at the Ministry of Sound for New Year's Eve. I left a nice party and good people at around midnight to make my way to join the Witch and her vampire friends. As soon as I showed up, she wanted to leave the club immediately, wasting thousands of pounds paid for the table and drinks. We went to a hotel suite she had hired for the night with her English friend as an observer. Whilst we travelled there in a taxi, she was on the phone and inviting some of the sleazy men who were sniffing around her to join us. She wanted to see how I would react to the pressure of this perverse situation. My protest was ignored and she was smiling from ear to ear thinking of the potential conflict, it was delicious to her.

When we arrived at the hotel, I just stood back and let the show unfold. I knew that I had the option to just walk out the door, but I sat down and made myself watch the sleazy men trying to make angles to get to her and push me out. They were dancing on the table and the Witch was feeding on being the centre of attention. I eventually got sick of what I was seeing, got up and left. The Witch acted like she was surprised on the surface, but she got exactly what she wanted. As I walked away from that hotel, I was upset and I felt stupid that I had allowed myself to be so easily drawn in and used. The advice and warnings that my friends gave me were clearly accurate, but I continued to be sucked in by her. Looking back now and with better knowledge, I can see that she was a psychopath. I am wondering if there was something in me that gravitated towards pleasing a psychopath, whilst ignoring the obvious evidence of destructive and parasitical behaviour.

I started 2007 with a determination to avoid the Witch, but she would not go away easily. She was an experienced shapeshifter who had moved to different cities and re-invented herself many times. She decided to play another game and pretend to be vulnerable and lonely. She told me that she wanted to get away from the parties and the bad people around her. Stupidly, I fell for it and I agreed to meet up, but it had to be just me and her. This was better for a little while, but she always managed to steer things to a place where large volumes of cocaine were involved. Back then I could handle cocaine, I could consume it for days and still function in some way. She knew what she was doing, she was luring me into deep waters.

The Witch started to increase her demands, phoning me in the middle of the night to instruct me to come to her apartment. This meant that I would leave in the morning after a night of cocaine madness and try to function and cover things at work. She had money and resources to avoid responsibility, but this situation was getting way too messy for me to handle. I wanted to get out and I started to ignore her calls, she did not like this. The tone between us moved in a more sinister direction. She told me that I had to see her, otherwise, she was going to tell her Russian boyfriend about me and that there would be serious consequences. She started to send me aggressive messages when she was drunk or high, which was almost daily. I was just waiting for something bad to happen.

One morning, I woke up to several missed calls and erratic messages from the Witch. Her voicemail stated that she was going to kill herself, I fell for her story and called her back. She was in her apartment, talking to me about trying to cut herself with a knife. I could then hear her on the balcony several floors up, it was very windy and she was trying to climb over the railing and jump to her death. She was out of her mind and screaming. I tried to calm her down and get her back into the apartment but she was not listening. She was unhinged and I was sure that she was going to jump. I kept her on the phone whilst I put my clothes on and prepared to drive to her apartment. When she realised that

I was on my way, she calmed down a little and went back inside and away from the balcony. She was delighted with the success of her new strategy.

I drove there a high speed, parked my car in the underground car park and made my way through the usual security doors, leaving clear evidence of my visit. I was stupid enough to think that I had no option but to save her from disaster. As I entered her apartment, the Witch standing still in the kitchen, there were small drops of blood on the wooden floor and a large kitchen knife with blood on it placed on the table. She was holding her wrist, and the window leading to the balcony was still wide open. It looked like a genuine suicide attempt, but it was staged to manipulate me.

I checked her wrist, but it was not the kind of focused and deep cut that could cause her to bleed to death. It was just a flesh wound. A small part of me started to think that maybe she was just looking for attention, but it was not the right moment to confront her. I closed the balcony door and recovered the bloodied knife that was placed on the table, leaving my fingerprints on it. We talked, she calmed down and seemed satisfied that she got what she wanted that morning. I left the apartment around lunchtime to go to work after contacting someone she knew to check on her. My relationship with the Witch was moving into a very dangerous space, and I wondered how I would escape. If she tried this stunt again and went further, I could be in the middle of a police investigation and on the wrong side of her Russian boyfriend. Fortunately for me, I did manage to break my ties with the Witch, but the protection I received came from tragedy.

13. Mammy is Taken

Mammy was poor and deprived for most of her life, but in her final years, she achieved some financial independence from my father. One of my sisters worked in the local golf club and she helped Mammy to secure a modest job washing dishes in the kitchen. Everybody in the golf club loved her, she had such an affinity with people of all ages. With a cup of tea and a cigarette in hand, chatting with the staff on her break, she was in her element. For the first time in her life, Mammy had a bank account and even a futuristic mobile phone. I used to tease her and ask her who she was calling and texting, she was far from being technology-minded. Mammy always put me in my place by saying “Your mother is full of surprises”, which was very true.

Every time I came back to Ireland to visit, Mammy wanted to demonstrate her newfound financial capability. Before I could say no, an all-out feast was laid on, beef, chicken, turkey, ham, cakes, desserts and much more than I could possibly eat. I repetitively told her that I couldn’t consume all of the food, but she insisted. The fridge was permanently empty when I was a child and this was her chance to show me that she was now a success as a mother and free from my father’s punitive financial control. The pleasure that she got from being able to give me more than just her love must have meant so much, even if it came in her seventies.

"Lightning Strike"

Mammy's older brother became sick in late 2006. He lived his entire life on his own in the family home where Mammy was born in rural County Limerick. When his death looked like a reality, problems started to emerge about the family home that would be left behind. Mammy put love before money and she was not equipped to deal with this kind of situation and politics. She did not articulate her feelings clearly, but I know that this greed hurt her deeply. My father did not help Mammy, but I found out that the Rebel was trying to support her during this conflict. When my uncle passed away, I knew I had to travel back to Ireland to provide a show of strength at the funeral.

My uncle was buried in the church grounds of his village. Many people attended the funeral, he was a funny and well-loved man. The priest who gave the service remarked that my uncle lived a solitary life, he never married. But the priest said that my uncle was a good man who loved to work in his garden, tending to his vegetables and surrounded by his animals. The priest then said something profound that has stuck with me. He said: "it's not about being in the front row of the church every Sunday, those who are close to nature, are close to God". This summed up my uncle perfectly, wedded to a simple life, in harmony with the earth and never taking too much.

After the church service, we all moved to the freshly dug grave in the church grounds. Several local men commenced the difficult task of lowering the coffin into the dark earth, whilst the priest said the holy words. This was the moment when Mammy realised her kind brother was gone from this world. She idolised him, he was always there for Mammy throughout her life, like a rock. Mammy suddenly broke down, tears violently erupted and she let out a scream of pure pain. Her body jolted and became contorted, it was like she was struck by a powerful bolt of lightning and it wounded her mortally. I know that my mother died a little that day.

Mammy was crying uncontrollably at the graveside, but nobody was helping her. Daddy just stood beside her and looked at her with a combination of confusion and annoyance. He was mainly concerned that people would see that he had no genuine instinct to help her. He did not even reach out a hand to comfort his wife. I was standing on the other side of the grave watching this tragic scene unfold. I didn't care about Catholic funeral etiquette, I broke free from the crowd and I ran around the grave to embrace Mammy and steady her little body before she fell to the ground. She looked like she wanted to follow her brother into the grave if I hadn't acted. I hugged her and I tried to absorb some of her pain, but the damage was done. Daddy remained unmoved, standing beside her but now he was looking away, relieved that I had handled his public embarrassment. His lack of empathy was never so stark.

Everyone went to the local village pub for a few drinks and sandwiches after the funeral. The tension was palpable, small tense groups gathered, sipped their drinks cautiously and avoided eye contact. It was interesting to see who supported Mammy in such a public setting. Of course, the Robot and the Rattlesnake were at the funeral and in the pub that day. My brother kept himself busy, making pointless small talk with strangers and avoiding his proper responsibilities. The Rattlesnake was working the room, laughing and grinning from ear to ear. She was chatting loudly and openly demonstrating her alliance with the people who were undermining my mother. This was an opportunity for the Rattlesnake, she could smell that Mammy was weakened and vulnerable.

Mammy asked me to take her to my uncle's house to spend some time there. This was her birthplace and I insisted that she was given access. Some family members who were close to my uncle also joined us. We stood in his stone kitchen and shared old and sweet stories about a warm man. He was also very funny, with a smile and a sparkle in his eyes that could entertain you without the need for words. Mammy said goodbye to her kind brother, he understood her and had helped her many times. This loss and the politics at the funeral left Mammy heartbroken, she looked like she had given up hope. Her reservoir of strength and hope was running low and her fragile little body was reaching its limitations. I travelled back to England after the funeral, but I was very worried about Mammy. I should have stayed longer to be with her.

"The Call"

I was at work on Thursday 15th February 2007, walking through the Finance department on my way to a meeting. At around 3 pm I saw an Irish number flash up on my mobile phone. I knew that something serious had happened because I never received calls from Ireland. One of my brothers told me that Mammy had a massive heart attack whilst she was at work and that she was in hospital in critical condition. I hung up and went straight into action mode, I had to be with her as soon as possible. I left the office immediately and drove home at speed whilst on the phone organising a flight to take me from London to Dublin and a taxi to get me to the airport. I arrived at my flat, ran inside and grabbed my passport, some spare clothes and a suit. I presumed that I would need the suit for a funeral, which made me feel guilty already. A few hours later, I was in Ireland and at

Mammy's hospital bedside. Nothing would have stopped me from getting there.

As I walked into the hospital ward, I was holding down many emotions and it was hard to take everything in. Mammy was lying on a bed, unresponsive and powered by a life support machine. It was likely that she had brain damage due to lack of oxygen after the heart attack. All of my brothers and sisters were there, nieces and nephews too. Everyone was traumatised, sibling conflicts were suspended for a while and there was a temporary cease-fire in place. However, one significant family member was missing, Daddy was not there. My brothers and sisters were talking about him, disgusted by his lack of care, but they were guarded in front of me. Daddy stayed away from the hospital because he needed to plan for his life after Mammy's death and how he was going to get through the funeral. He knew that emotions would be high and there would be the potential for public confrontation. He waited at home to think through his game plan and for my arrival at the hospital to guarantee his safety.

About one hour later, Daddy suddenly walked into the hospital ward. He was very calm, but his presence made my siblings tense. I greeted him with enthusiasm to try and smooth over a difficult situation. Daddy immediately started to control the situation and unnerve people. One of my sisters was standing very close to Mammy's bedside and rubbing her hands and feet. She knew that Mammy would want her eyebrows lined whilst she was so defenceless and everyone was looking at her.

She put a little make-up on Mammy and made a joke about it. This irritated Daddy, he was mocking and dismissive. He leaned in and gave orders, "Stop doing that to your mother, leave her alone". But my sister snarled at him and he backed off to avoid being embarrassed.

Things were very tense in the ward, I was waiting for an emotional outburst or anger from some direction. Daddy asked me to come for a walk with him, some fresh air was a good idea, but this was not a spontaneous act. We walked down the road and I chatted nervously about my life in England. Daddy listened and he was strangely interested. I told him that I was thinking of moving to London to get away from my flat and boring life in a commuter town outside London. Surprisingly, he offered to give me some money to help with the move, but he told me not to mention it to anyone. Such an act seemed to be fatherly and thoughtful, but now I know differently. When he received the news of Mammy's massive heart attack, he sat down at home for hours to carefully select who was the most useful and how to navigate the situation. I was the obvious choice and he knew that I would be sucked in by the cash gift.

The Robot and the Rattlesnake were also in the hospital that evening. My pointless brother had his head down and provided no emotional value to anyone. The Rattlesnake was slithering around in the background, trying very hard not to stand too close to Mammy's bedside or be caught locking eyes with Daddy. I had not yet accepted that the affair between Daddy and the

Rattlesnake was a reality. If I had been awake, as I am today, I would have banished both of them from the ward. Neither of them wanted to be there for any good reason. I could sense most of my siblings did not want the Rattlesnake to be there, but she stuck around, driven by her ambition to reconnect with Daddy when Mammy was gone.

In this extreme crisis, siblings started to talk to each other and new information came to the surface. I found out that Mammy had survived at least one smaller heart attack during the previous year. One of my brothers personally witnessed the attack. He said that he saw her barely able to stand and gasping for air, but she called out, “Not now, not now”, as she fought to stay alive.

Mammy was close to God and she lived a very spiritual life. Maybe her greatest fear was knowing that when she would leave this world, her children and grandchildren would suffer. We also found out that she had been told by her doctor in her final years that she urgently needed a heart bypass operation, but she hid this medical fact from everyone. Daddy was aware of her minor heart attack, but he didn't care enough to investigate her true health condition. If she became incapacitated, this would just be an inconvenience for him. Mammy knew that it was just a matter of time before she would be taken by a heart attack.

"Masterpiece"

Mammy hung on for a few days but the doctors did not understand how she kept going. Her vital signs were deteriorating and her organs were failing. Only a rhythmic and ghostly life support machine was keeping her alive and morphine was numbing her pain. We were all at Mammy's bedside on Sunday 18th February, her children, her grandchildren and even Daddy and the Rattlesnake. The nurse told us to be prepared for her to go, but she hung on. Why was she being so stubborn? We then realised that one of my sisters was missing. The last few days had been very traumatic and we had all drifted in and out of the hospital, hardly eating or sleeping. One of my sisters had gone for a drive to isolate herself, this was her way of coping and she had not yet come back to the hospital that afternoon. We hoped that she would make it there in time, but she not responding to calls and text messages.

The afternoon pressed on, and Mammy's blood pressure was on the floor, the nurses could not believe that she was holding on. She was clinging to her life and waiting so that everyone would be with her in the end. The missing sister suddenly walked into the ward and joined us and there was a sense of collective relief. Most of us felt guilty that we wanted Mammy to pass, but we agreed that a life with no brain activity on a life support machine was not our mother. In front of everyone, I got down on one knee and took Mammy by the hand and said: "We are all here now, it's time to go". Within seconds she slipped away gently.

The nurses pulled the curtains, switched off the machines, and encouraged us to leave the body with them. Most of the family cried, some walked away quickly, overcome with emotion, and some tried to stay by her bedside to say a final goodbye. Daddy retreated to the waiting room to isolate himself and avoid any anger that could be aimed at him. My first instinct in the aftermath was to protect my father and I joined him in the waiting room. We were alone and he started talking in a very low and strange voice. He was not directing it at me, he was talking whilst looking away into the distance, like a rehearsal. Daddy admitted that he did not treat Mammy very well, but he blamed his father, who had passed down to him a "genetic bad character". Daddy then just spat out an unexpected confession. He started to talk about the secret baby that Mammy lost as a frightened teenager in

London in the late 1940s and that he was the father. It sounded like he wanted to cover his tracks in some way, just in case it came up after she was gone. Daddy was lining up and rehearing his excuses to justify more than fifty years of domination and abuse.

"Handbag Trophy"

It was clear that Daddy was not upset and he didn't want to be consoled. I started to think about the rest of the family and I went outside to the car park where everyone was gathered in little splinter groups. When I left Daddy alone in the waiting room the Rattlesnake immediately slithered in and made herself available to serve his needs. Mammy's body had not yet gone cold, but Rattlesnake could not wait to get started. My father now had more practical and self-serving tasks in mind, he wanted to get hold of Mammy’s handbag to access her modest little bank account. He also wanted to see what other secrets she had in her closely protected handbag. Unbelievably, the Rattlesnake's first task to prove her loyalty was to retrieve Mammy’s handbag for him.

One of my sisters grabbed Mammy’s handbag from the bedside when she passed. She knew that Daddy would immediately try to seize any assets. I was standing in the car park when I saw the Rattlesnake walk out from the hospital and brazenly say “The Boss wants your mother’s handbag”. My sister went fucking crazy, shouting, barking, snapping, shaking with anger, but this did not deter the Rattlesnake. I saw the confrontation but I didn’t fully understand what was going on. My instinct was to stop any fighting just after Mammy died. I got angry with my sister and quelled the confrontation. Mammy's handbag was reluctantly handed over, with me as the enforcer, I am ashamed to say. The Rattlesnake quickly slithered back to Daddy and passed over the goods.

With the handbag secure, Daddy went home immediately and carefully went through the contents. Official documents were separated from the sentimental items. Mammy was made to sign various insurance policies over the years without explanation, and now it was time to profit from her death. The sentimental items were thrown to one side, including the letters that I wrote to Mammy when I first ran away to England. Mammy had even kept an emotional letter that I had written to Daddy when I was trying to rebuild my relationship with him. He discarded my letter when he first received it, and now he was discarding it for a second time. I got my hands on those letters and I took them away to read them privately. I destroyed the letter that I wrote to Daddy, knowing that he did not respond to it. The letters that I wrote to Mammy were in perfect condition, she kept them in a plastic bag to preserve them over the years. These letters will be with me forever.

Whilst Daddy was busy in the kitchen organising documents and calculating profits, I went to the front room to be alone. This room was always a place that I retreated to for isolation when I was upset as a child. Daddy was enjoying his own company and he even prepared a hearty meal for one, he had not lost his appetite. Mammy kept many sentimental objects linked to her children and her grandchildren in the front room. She decorated this cold room with photos, artwork, sports trophies, jewellery, trinkets and newspaper cuttings mentioning my name after football matches. It was comforting to be around these connections to Mammy, I could feel her spirit close by.

"Russian Danger"

My mobile phone suddenly rang, it was the Witch calling me from London. This unexpected call should have unnerved me, but I immediately knew that Mammy's death was going to protect me. I answered the call happily, knowing that I was about to get that vicious woman out of my life permanently. The Witch asked me if I wanted to come over to her place that night. I took my time and teased out the conversation, informing her that I was in Ireland, but I gave her no further information. She quickly realised that I was not useful to her on that specific evening. That was my first move before I landed the killer blow. Curiosity drove her to ask me why I was in Ireland. I allowed a short silence before speaking to make sure that her ears were primed and ready. I then said, “My mother has died today and I need to be in Ireland with my family”. There was a long silence.

The Witch did not expect this, I could feel her thinking in the distance. She was already selecting more useful alternatives, I was now completely useless to her. After a prolonged silence, she then gave me a very disingenuous message of sympathy, but she was already distancing herself, she couldn’t wait to end the call. I just stayed silent, pretending that I wanted to keep the call going and I needed emotional support. She said she would call me when I was back in London, but I continued to stay on the phone, holding my silence but smiling inside. I wanted her to back out of the conversation. Her final words to me were "Take care" before she hung up abruptly. I looked up to the heavens and said "Thank you Mammy". Even in her death, she was protecting me from danger.

"Cold Monday"

Daddy woke up Monday morning with a specific task in mind. He went to the bank as soon as it was opened to access Mammy's account. However, he got a slap in the face when he was informed by the bank that he was not her nominated next of kin. One of my sisters anticipated this outcome when she set up the bank account for Mammy. She assigned a different next of kin to block Daddy when the inevitable would happen. Daddy was furious that he could not add her humble savings to his wealth. He even tried to cash her final pay cheque from the golf club that he found in the bottom of her handbag, but it was in her name and this was also rejected by the bank. Undeterred, I was told that Daddy went to the golf club a couple of weeks later and compelled the manager to make out a new pay cheque for Mammy's work in his name. It is hard to contemplate that a husband could be so heartless.

Siblings needed to come together to organise the funeral, this was not going to be easy. We had very strained and inconsistent relationships with each other. Most had not talked for years and some could not be in the same room together. My role was to be the referee and the bouncer to maintain order. I also had the responsibility of keeping Daddy updated. I tried to encourage him to get involved, but he didn't want to know. We got together in my sister's home. This was the first and only time that all of the siblings talked at one table. After an emotional start, we did manage to make some plans and assign different roles to get the job done. Organise a priest, buy flowers and let people know the date and time, there was much to do. Bodies are buried within a few days in Ireland. It was all hands to the deck with no time to think about grief.

"Happy Birthday"

The funeral date was 21st February, my birthday. Throughout my childhood, celebrations were stamped on by Daddy which made me reluctant to enjoy birthdays fully. But now I like this bitter-sweet connection to Mammy's life every year, it keeps her close to me. My siblings gathered in our family home, but most of them had not been there for years. That house reminded them of Daddy, betrayal, conflict, violence, and it took Mammy's death to force us to stand in the same room. Daddy requested all of us to be there before the church. We stood in the front room, heads down, waiting for the master of the house to talk. His very first words were not spontaneous, he said: "This is the last time we will all be together". One of my brothers tried to say something to soften the situation, but he was immediately told to "Shut up" very forcibly. Daddy was controlling the situation to ensure his reputation would not be impacted negatively. Emotions and grief were a threat, his children could lash out at him in public. He then said "make your mother proud in the church", which translated to "Don't embarrass me ". We were dismissed.

The long black funeral cars transported the family to the church. When we arrived, Mammy's body was waiting outside at the bottom of the steps. As per tradition, the men in the family were expected to carry her coffin into the church and up to the altar. Daddy avoided getting involved, so, I quickly organised a group comprised of some sons and grandsons. I was at the back of the formation of six, encouraging the men to link arms and embrace awkwardly to take the weight of her coffin on our shoulders. The church was packed, every seat was taken and the back and sides were full of people standing. This church was a place that Mammy frequented very often, she loved to light candles and pray quietly. It was her sanctuary and spiritual home. The sons and grandsons stepped together cautiously down the church aisle and her body was laid down in front of the altar. What a pity that we waited for her funeral to lift her up high and honour this woman.

I had been away in England for many years, but I still recognised some of the local faces paying their respects. There were also faces that I did not recognise, Mammy had many friends and she was quietly helping people in their struggles. The family took our place in the front rows and I strategically positioned myself next to

Daddy as his bodyguard. I was standing between him and his children and their collective hatred towards him. We had lost Mammy and now they despised him even more for the miserable life he had given her. I was so preoccupied with protecting Daddy, that it did not even register with me that I had suffered a loss.

One of my brothers wrote a poem for Mammy with very touching words. It describes a lady surviving a tough life gracefully and being an inspiration to her family. My brother stood at the front of the entire church and he read his poem to hundreds of people. The words rang through the crowd like a bell, the truth in that poem made you cry and laugh at the same time. Everyone was so moved that when the poem ended, the entire church broke into a spontaneous and loud applause. Such a joyous response was unusual at an Irish Catholic funeral, but we all felt it. Nothing could contain the love that poured out from everyone who knew her. However, Daddy had not authorised the poem and I could see from his thunderous face that he was not happy about the response it received.

Despite the loss, it seems strange to say, but I enjoyed the funeral. It was the funeral that Mammy deserved and it had a sense of joy and celebration. Everything went so perfectly, the huge crowds, the moving poem, the applause, the endless queue of people wanting to shake our hands to offer their condolences. Mammy got her grand farewell in the place where she was most at peace. After the church service, we all followed her coffin to the graveyard and we watched silently as her body was lowered into the earth. Daddy kept his head down and separated himself. The church service had passed over successfully and he knew that the finishing line was close. One of my sisters threw a pack of Mammy's favourite cigarettes into the grave as they started to shovel the soil onto the coffin. I was waiting for Mammy to push open the coffin lid, grab the cigarettes and quickly squirrel them inside before Daddy could notice. Some smokes would be helpful to keep her going on the journey.

After Mammy's body was laid to rest, many people joined the family at the golf club where she used to work for drinks and food. I was mostly guarding Daddy, sticking by his side, to make sure there was no drama or unwanted confrontations that would spoil the occasion. But I did get a chance to speak to one specific woman who worked with Mammy. She was staring directly into my eyes and trying to work out who I was within the family. When she realised I was the youngest child she said "Oh, so you are her baby who ran away to England". She had connected my face with the stories that Mammy had shared with her. She told me that Mammy had said that I always "looked after her", despite being away. I am very grateful that this woman found a way to tell me this precious piece of information. It keeps me warm and gives me strength.

People drifted away politely as the afternoon pressed on. I could see that Daddy was becoming agitated, he wanted to get out of there. Arrangements were made to drive him home and I headed to the airport to get back to England. My duty was done and now I wanted to escape to my own lonely corner and lick my wounds. When my flight landed in London later that evening I felt relief, the pressure was off. I thought that I could now start to deal with the loss, but I was not ready or willing to face it. Perhaps I could run for a while, but eventually, the grief and the hurt would catch up with me and bring me to my knees.

14. Falling Down

I really noticed how cold and hollow my flat was when I arrived after my flight from Ireland. It was expensively furnished, but it was a sterile and lonely home. In the aftermath of Mammy's death, I was completely numb. Inevitably, I went out to a club in Vauxhall that Saturday night to escape from myself. I had some party friends back then who were trying to offer me care, but I was not able to accept their help. I was trying to laugh off their efforts and they didn't know what to do with me. The invincible hero show was deployed to block their help and I went out to get high and forget everything. Many familiar faces approached me in the club and asked me "How are you?". I just told them straight, "My mother died last weekend". My response to their intended sociable gesture shocked people and killed the mood, but I was doing it on purpose.

"Best Friend"

I took several ecstasy pills on that Saturday night, but it was not working. I could not get high and there was no rush of serotonin. Euphoria was not possible, there was a complete mental block. Despite the obvious evidence that I was not getting high, I took some more pills. This was now getting very dangerous, I didn't come up or get high, instead, my body started to shake, I was sweating, light-headed and nauseous. There were two possible options when ecstasy is making you sick:

Option 1, try to vomit to get the toxic chemicals out of your system.

Option 2, take a very strong line of cocaine and the powerful stimulant will hopefully numb the feeling of being sick.

Predictably, I went for option 2. I straightened up and I got back to the party person that I needed to be to get through that night and weekend. If I was high, I could avoid thinking about the loss and processing the grief.

My use of cocaine was progressing silently in the background for a couple of years, but it was not yet fully in control. When I opted for cocaine to help after the loss of Mammy, something changed and I became a different man. The happy party drug Ecstasy was left behind and would never work for me again. A new connection was formed with a stronger, more expensive and more addictive drug. Cocaine was now my first choice for medicine and a miracle cure when I was in trouble. I had found a new best friend and it came before everything. Despite trying to hide the true excesses of my developing addiction, I soon developed a reputation and I was using more white powder than anyone I knew. Everywhere I went, I had some cocaine secured deeply in a discreet pocket. I even bought clothes with the consideration of how effective the pocket structure would be to conceal and keep dry my critical supply.

If I was going to a party or club, I would not leave home without cocaine in my pocket, or I would be 100% sure that I could access it there. I was also getting fussy about quality. This was not because I wanted value for money, it was because only the strongest cocaine would work for me. I was taking so much that my tolerance level required the kind of purity that scared other people. The smell was enough for me to assess the strength. If I didn't like the smell of any cocaine offered to me at a party, I would refuse to even try it, knowing that the lack of quality would only frustrate me and I would be trapped in a halfway place desperately looking for a stronger version. I was like a fine wine connoisseur, looking down my nose at those who foolishly indulged in poor quality powder.

“Work Sabotage”

I went back to work immediately after Mammy passed. I did not ask for time off to recover and start the grieving process properly. It is not surprising that I became agitated and withdrawn at work. I was picking fights with various senior managers and directors, looking for trouble. Something was driving me to sabotage the career success that I had worked so hard for. Despite the partying in recent years, I had managed to keep work going and nobody could deny that my department had delivered results. But I was now tipping the balance in the wrong direction. Forcing people to deal with my dysfunctional behaviour was my way of hurting myself. I wanted the world to come crashing down on top of me. Monday became “working from home”, this was code for recovering in bed, usually with some random girl from the weekend. Tuesdays to Thursdays were a struggle, trying badly to be productive, but I was way off the pace and people were noticing. Sometimes the weekend started early, going out on Thursday night because I was too impatient to wait for Friday.

There was a report from head office that my phone bill was the highest in the company for usage outside of office hours. Most of my calls were after midnight, which is hard to explain as "business use". There were frequent damage bills from accidents in my company car going from club to party across London. Colleagues had to witness the carnage and some even helped to cover things at times, making excuses to directors who were looking for me. I had built up a great team, but I was distracted by what was going on in my personal life. I know that many of my team thought highly of me and if things had been different, I could have done more for them, but it was not the right time. I am thankful that some of those colleagues who tried to help are still my friends now and they can witness me acknowledging my mistakes in this story.

I met a friend for dinner on a Thursday night in central London and we ordered cocaine for dessert afterwards. Once we were a few lines in, I left my friend and drove home high as a kite. Something was pushing me to go on and on, and I started to drink heavily when I arrived back to my flat. This developed into a party for one, putting on flashy new clothes and sunglasses, dancing solo in front of the large mirror in my hallway and chatting with myself. What a sad vision of a man. My next bad decision was to drive back into London to go to Vauxhall on my own. As I cruised through the streets of West London, I became more aware that I was driving intoxicated and the risk of being caught by the police was on my mind. I quickly dumped my car on a side street and hailed a passing taxi to take me to Fire.

I was manic when I entered Fire, aggressively pushing through the doors to join the crowd in the main room. I dived into more cocaine and alcohol, with no thought of how I would deal with tomorrow. The club was busy and I recognised many familiar faces, but people were behaving differently around me. I was not getting the same reaction, girls were avoiding my advances and strangers were stepping around me, I was giving off a very different energy. I was a cocaine monster, frenzied, sleazy, rude and a person that you needed to avoid if you wanted to have fun. I stayed in Fire all night, but the club was closing at 8 am and I was one of the last people to leave. I was wired out of my mind as I hit the street and daylight. My car had already been impounded for parking illegally in a residential street and I had also managed to lose my keys, mobile phone and wallet.

"Mr Soldier"

I was fortunate enough to have a right-hand man at work who is still a very close friend. Mr Soldier was an army man in his youth, disciplined, loyal and very trustworthy. He was the best person to get me out of this corner. I had a small amount of cash and coins on me, so

I jumped into a taxi to central London. I called him from a pay phone and got straight to the point. I said, “I am fucked, book me a hotel”, and I gave Mr Soldier the name of a hotel that I could see across the street. I ended the call and we arranged to speak in ten minutes to obtain the booking information. He was shocked and unsettled by my desperate call, but he immediately sprang into action. As promised, I called him back from the same coin box, but he was struggling to sort out the room booking. I was nervous and I needed to get off the busy and noisy street. Direct action was required to deal with this emergency.

I walked straight into the target hotel, ignored the long queue and I picked up the phone at the reception desk. I called Mr Soldier and when he answered, I handed the phone to the Scandinavian looking guy working in reception. He was shocked by my directness but he stayed calm. Mr Soldier and the reception guy talked on the phone, but both were struggling with this odd situation that I forced on them. My dramatic performance was also upsetting the Friday morning routine for the business guests queuing up to check out, they were staring at me with open mouths. To lighten the mood, I joked loudly that my friend used to be in the military and that he should be skilled in dealing with "life and death situations". I was looking for attention, but I was the only person who laughed at this poorly timed joke.

Mr Soldier finally managed to pay for a room with his credit card and I was handed the key to get me out of reception as quickly as possible. I got myself into the room, lay on the bed and I tried to sleep, but it was impossible. When I closed my eyes there were strange noises inside my head. It sounded like distressed and contorted voices crunched together, grinding, screeching, nonsensical high-pitched noises. These violent noises were communicating some kind of condemnation of my spirit, a message of doom, filling my head with desperate squeals and groans of pain. I couldn't sleep, I couldn't cry, I couldn't let go. I was exhausted and I didn't know how I would fix this mess.

I stayed in the hotel room for a couple of restless hours but I could not escape how I was feeling. A friend of mine worked in a shop a couple of miles away. I planned to borrow some money from her and get a train home. It was raining as I applied myself to the necessary walk through the busy streets of London. This cooled me down and slowly calmed me, I was thankful for the rain that morning. Walking has always helped me, step by step, slowly getting to somewhere better. I was observing the chaos of city life as I passed each street. Focused business people going to their next meeting, fashionable girls floating into boutiques and working-class men telling loud jokes in slow-moving white vans. Part of me felt lost and alone in this confusing world. But there was also a voice telling me that I must try to keep going.

"Pushed Out"

There were some structure changes at work at that time and the department of thirty people that I had built up was going to be cut by ten positions. People with real lives, families, homes and mortgages would lose their jobs. The other part of the change was that the board of directors wanted me to leave my position, I had run out of their support. I had blurted out too many sarcastic and barbed comments in the presence of self-important egos, instead of bowing my head and laughing at their jokes. I was looking for trouble and they had seen my behaviour go in the wrong direction after the death of Mammy. I was a liability to them now and they were willing to pay me off for a quick exit and push me out the door.

My emotions and loyalties in this situation were very torn. I knew that I was no longer welcome and it would have been easy to walk away with some quick money, but I asked to stay on to personally manage the restructuring. I wanted to make sure that the right people kept their jobs, and I wanted to look those people that I had to let go in the eyes and be honest with them. It was hard but it had to be me. The loss of Mammy and the loss of my own job were put on hold, and I got on with the unenviable task of terminating people. The structure changes were finalised in the summer of 2007 and I left work quietly. I felt guilty about my role in the whole situation. But it was a relief to walk away and get some cash to opt out of normal life for a while.

Around this time, I was experiencing terrifying nightmares so vivid that I feared going to bed at night. Spirits were visiting me to pass on some kind of message that I didn't understand. I had the very real sensation of someone pressing down on me with an impossible weight whilst I was trapped in my sleep, a weight so heavy that I could not move my body. I also dreamt of people sitting on my bed, a man and woman whom I did not recognise, pulling my arms in opposite directions, trying to tear me apart. It kept happening night after night and I didn't know how to make it stop. I decided to sell my flat, grab the available cash and move into a rented shared house in central London with some party friends.

"Party House"

My new home was a modern townhouse with three levels. A bonus for me was a private entrance on the ground through patio doors leading directly into my bedroom and my own bathroom. My housemate's rooms, the dining room and the kitchen were all located upstairs on the higher levels. This was very convenient, I could slip in and out unnoticed and conceal my behaviour.

Another critical advantage was the location. The clubs in Vauxhall were quickly accessible via a short walk. There were also other unexpected benefits to shared living. Group dinners and friendly faces calling around on a regular basis helped to take away some of my loneliness in the short term.

My use of cocaine at home started to accelerate in this new location. Whilst everyone else was at work, I would call my dealer and get a quick delivery. Before this stage, I would generally only use cocaine to go out in the evening time and at clubs and parties. Now I was having solo cocaine binges in my bedroom on a Tuesday afternoon. I would lock myself away, doing lines, knocking back whisky, listening to music, dancing, watching porn, anything to hide away in my own twisted and toxic world. As I started to increase the level of cocaine, staying confined in my bedroom became difficult. I was constantly "missing in action", walking around London, stopping at random pubs, bars and strip clubs to get a stiff drink to take the edge off and hang out for a while. The people who worked there looked at me as someone who was easy to extract money from. Respectable places were not an option, only the dives and seedy backstreet bars accepted my presence.

"Hammer Blow"

Fire on a Sunday afternoon was a great place if you wanted to chill out. I often went there to wind down after an exhausting marathon over Friday and Saturday night. I was sitting at a table outside in the garden area, chatting with two middle-aged gay men and a very loud woman. The gay guys were nice, social and welcoming, but the loud woman was a different story. She was about thirty, with big blond hair, partly attractive, oversized tacky sunglasses, heavily branded designer clothes and a big mouth to match her vulgar appearance. The gay guys suddenly announced that they were going to another club and asked me to come along. It was just across the street, a five-minute walk and I had nothing better to do.

We walked along the busy Vauxhall roads whilst normal people went about their Sunday afternoon business. We passed families with small kids going for dinner, cyclists and joggers out exercising and people travelling via the station. The gay guys were walking ahead and the loud woman and I had fallen behind. She was talking shit and unaware of whether I was even listening. There was a one-way stream of arrogant and crude noise coming out of her mouth and very little contribution from me. Suddenly and without warning, she asked me an unexpected question. She said: "What would your mother think about that?" I responded factually by saying "My mother died earlier this year". She then said the words that triggered something that I was not prepared for. Without looking at me she said "You know nothing about loss".

The world instantly froze, I stopped walking and everything went quiet. I let the gay guys and the loud woman walk off into the distance. The harshness of her response was enough to take all the fight out of me. I had suppressed the pain with cocaine and denial for too long and my grief hit me all at once. Mammy is dead. I burst into tears violently. The tears flowed down my face so hard that I could not see in front of me. My legs suddenly lost their power and I fell to the ground for a moment. In desperation, I got to my feet and stumbled into a nearby empty bus stop shelter. Better to hide and allow the volcanic groans of pain to explode. As I stood in the bus shelter, shaking and crying, a sudden summer rainstorm started with a loud bang of thunder. Then came flashes of lighting and a downpour of monsoon-like rain fell from the heavens.

Someone up high could see my tragic soul crying in the bus shelter and they sent the storm to cloak me. Soon there was a torrent of rainwater rushing down the city roads, flooding the drains and hiding my tears from the people passing by and running for cover. The overwhelming pain inside of me and the raw electricity from the storm fused together for a moment. I have never felt such a powerful force. When the intense rain eased off, people started to move around again. A sweet girl that I knew from the clubs walked past and stopped to take a second look. She realised that I was crying, she approached cautiously and offered to help. Despite my protests of "I am fine", she made me join her in another club for the remainder of that afternoon and evening. I was glad of the support but I couldn't talk, I just took a seat and consumed more cocaine and alcohol. Later that night, I somehow found the energy to get to my feet and walk home. I arrived exhausted, drained of everything and beaten into submission.

"Dark Thoughts"

When I was recovering the morning after a cocaine binge, I would frequently have very clear thoughts of suicide as a quick way to escape and solve my problems. I even researched the best way to do it on the internet. There seemed to be no hope and I had backed myself into a corner. A good party friend that I had at that time told me something that helped me to turn back from such a serious step. He said: "Your mother fought so hard to give her children life, why would you just throw that away?". He was right, I needed to cling to Mammy's love and strength to save myself. Thoughts of suicide lingered menacingly for a while, but those dark motivations eventually drifted away. No matter how low, depressed and scared I became, an important part of me still tried to struggle forward.

Autumn arrived and the thrill of the weekend crowds going out on warm summer nights faded. Evenings were getting darker and the mood was changing. Despite the cloud of cocaine that enveloped me, I still understood that I needed to get a job. My cash ran out fast and a mountain of debt was growing bigger by the day with no money coming in. On paper, I had a good security career and it was possible to find a job. But I had zero motivation to put myself out there and I was not in the right place to contend with interviews. However, a company who had shown interest in recruiting my talent more than once came calling. My career had caught their eye and they had seen me present on stage at an industry conference. It was not the right organisation for me and I had said no to them before, but I needed a job.

"Tense Interview"

A formal interview was arranged for a Friday morning, but of course, I went out on Thursday night. I got around two hours of very bad sleep, jumped out of bed in a frantic state and threw on my suit and tie. To make matters worse, just before I left home, I had a massive line of cocaine to "pick me up". The effect seemed great for about twenty minutes, however, I became very nervous and edgy as I battled through London at peak time and my train journey to their office. When I finally arrived following a nightmare journey, I was twitching and sweating. But I had to face the meeting and try to smile at the director and human resources manager interviewing me. We made small talk and they asked me the obvious questions. I was completely unprepared and answered spontaneously and badly. My body movements and my face must have at least looked suspicious. That was the longest interview of my life.

I don't know how I got away with it, but I managed to get through the first interview and they asked me to come back for a second stage in the process. Even more ridiculous, but not that surprising considering my track record, I also went out the night before the planned second interview. I got so high on cocaine that I did not even show up. Self-sabotage was my operating system and I was pushing my life into a dark corner. I was now struggling to pay rent, unable to pay loans, multiple credit cards maxed and I was borrowing money from friends. Every time that I managed to get my hands on some cash, instead of buying food or paying an important bill, I got on the phone to a drug dealer. I felt like I had ruined my life, there was no way back, so I might as well get high to escape for a while.

Reluctantly, I signed on to receive government unemployment benefits. When you have nothing and you are desperate, you can appreciate the value of any small amount of cash in your pocket. I remember waiting for my benefit money to come through to my bank account on Monday morning, a modest £50. I went out walking late Sunday night to position myself close to a club and wait for Sunday night to become Monday morning at midnight. I walked manically through random London streets, counting down the minutes. As expected, my zero bank balance was improved by £50 just after midnight. I took that cash straight to a club where I knew I could get in for free and access a drug dealer. I purchased a single gram of cocaine and I ran home immediately to consume it. Addiction was driving me to neglect my basic need for food and shelter. It's hard to think that an intelligent person could do this and it's even harder to contemplate that it was me, but it was. This should have snapped me out of my behaviour, unfortunately, my addiction continued for many more years and it would bring me to even lower places.

"Work Frontier"

Despite being high on coke during the first interview and not showing up at the second interview, the company that wanted to recruit me were still open to a discussion. I gave them a story about being unsure of my career direction to recover the situation. I attended the next planned interview sober and secured a very well-paid job. Victory was pulled out of the jaws of death at the very last minute. I started working there in January 2008, hoping for a fresh start but my new job began very badly. I was unstable and I struggled to adapt to the new work environment and corporate culture. Once again, I deliberately found ways of not fitting in and sabotaging the situation. Conflict at work became my new frontier and battlefront. Anxiety drove me to invite unnecessary fights with work peers and I was over-sensitive in very normal scenarios. Work meetings were very stressful and

I hated every single moment. I felt isolated and it was highly likely that I would indulge in a cocaine binge later that evening. If we had a two-day meeting, sometimes I would fail to turn up for the second day because I had a cocaine binge overnight.

Relationships in the shared house in central London became very strained. I was not the fun guy they knew from before. The good times were officially over and I became the unwelcome guest. Tension was building under the surface and eventually, there was a big row. True to form, I over-reacted and I moved every piece of furniture out whilst my housemates were at work. They came home that evening to a completely bare house. No sofa, no table, no TV and not even a fork to eat with. All of the furniture was mine and everything came with me to my new flat in leafy North London. This area was much calmer and a long way from the Vauxhall clubs. A new and improved environment should have helped me to change, but in reality, my addiction got worse. My world revolved around making sure that I was always in a position to access cocaine. The weeks, months and years in that flat and job just slipped by. I was trapped in a twilight zone of progressive addiction and self-destruction.

15. Facing the Truth

After Mammy passed, Daddy lived on his own and I made regular trips to Ireland to support him. However, there was still a gap for an opportunist to slither her way back into his life. The Rattlesnake wasted no time letting him know that she was keen to be in the picture again. Home-cooked meals were prepared and delivered by the Robot to demonstrate her eagerness to re-ignite the old flame. The Robot was also instructed to carry out chores to help Daddy around the house and garden, and he complied as directed. Her greed and his son's submissive behaviour amused Daddy and he allowed the relationship to develop again. It could be useful and he was happy to have options.

Daddy viewed his sisters as superior to his own family. He telephoned them weekly, one in London and one in America, and he always complained about his own children. During a visit, I overheard the conversation with one of his sisters. He was playing the victim, saying "I just don't know what I have done wrong as a father". They believed his lies and he was invited to stay with them and go on holiday. In the summer of 2007, they toured around America, Ireland and England. This was a holiday to leave his life with Mammy behind and mark his new independent life. The final part of his celebration tour was in London and I drove to his sister's house to spend some time with him and bring him to the airport to travel back to Ireland.

When I walked into the house there was no real eye contact with me and I sensed a strange atmosphere. I encountered my father playing happy family with his sisters and the extended group. They were discussing holiday experiences and the famous sights they had seen. Daddy was posing for photos in his American clothes, baseball cap and branded polo shirt. He was an unrecognisable tourist cliché. Who was this strange new man? His sisters did not come to Mammy's funeral and nobody mentioned her death. There were when no condolences or "sorry for your loss" comments. I was annoyed, so, I just threw Mammy's death into the conversation to get a reaction. Daddy shook his head disappointingly and gave me a vicious look, I was not authorised to bring this up. Everybody just looked at the floor and stayed quiet.

Daddy had two major surgeries after Mammy died, a heart bypass and a hip replacement a couple of years later. He knew that he needed some of his children to help him recover after both operations. I was always his first choice and I travelled back to Ireland to assist. My sisters and a couple of my nieces also got involved and tried to help. It was gritty work, but we did it because of our collective respect for Mammy. One of my nieces told me that she was tasked with washing him in the shower. Whilst she focused on this repulsive task, he stood there naked, unembarrassed and delivered a steady stream of vicious insults to her face. It was always unpleasant dealing with him, you just had to look away and close your ears.

After the success of the major surgeries, Daddy was soon back doing all of the things that he enjoyed. Tending to his vegetables, walking the dogs, cutting firewood and driving to town to flirt with the pretty girls in the bank. His health and mobility improved significantly, he was like a younger man. During one trip home, I was watching him in the garden, he was down on his knees planting small cabbages in neat holes in the ground. He was moving quickly and seemingly without any pain. I stared at him for a minute and I could tell he knew that I was observing him. I said: “your new hip is working very well”, Daddy just nodded and continued without looking at me. But he was irritated and he realised that I was becoming suspicious and starting to see his underlying nature.

My weekly telephone call to Ireland became more and more difficult as the years passed. This was Daddy's opportunity to vent his hatred for his children, he mocked my brothers and sisters, jeering at their lives and struggles. I always tried to sit on the fence during these conversations or change the subject. If I defended them I was subsequently attacked, "Oh, so you are on their side". He labelled his children as "failures" and "wasters" and provided his evidence as to why that was the case. As the years passed, I learned to just hold the phone handset away from my ear, I was starting to disconnect from him and I was tired of trying to keep the peace.

Daddy was paranoid about home security after Mammy died and he was living on his own. He purchased a young female German Shepherd to protect the house. However, she was not an effective guard dog. His hostile nature penetrated her nervous system and affected her development. She was constantly shaking with fear and she lacked the confidence to match her physical appearance. The house had a dark and creepy atmosphere, it was missing Mammy's love and it was hard to sleep there. Daddy destroyed the room that he shared with Mammy. The bed was smashed and turned on its side and the carpets were ripped up and left strewn across the room. I tried to tidy up the house on every visit but it was obvious that he liked the filth and chaos. Not thinking that it would be a problem, I took a couple of photos of

Mammy back to England after one trip. When I telephoned Daddy to let him know I had landed safely after my flight, he immediately accused me of "stealing family property". My patience and my support for my father was starting to wear thin.

My final visit to Ireland to see Daddy whilst he was alive was in the summer of 2013. I borrowed his car one evening to visit one of my sisters, she had some serious health problems at that time and I had not seen her in a while. Despite Daddy's jealousy and disapproval, we spent some quality time together and I stayed late to catch up properly. When I arrived home, Daddy interrogated me, he wanted to know why I was late and exactly where I was. This was shocking, I said, "You know where I was". He said that he was going to check the mileage of the car to find out whether I was telling the truth. This was an official investigation. I informed him that his daughter had health problems, but he insulted her with mocking judgements about her life. Knowing that I would say too much, I bit my tongue and backed off temporarily. I went to bed immediately to get out of his way, but it was obvious that things were coming to a head. I forced myself to sleep that night, part of me hoped that the next day would be better, but most of me knew that a conflict was inevitable.

I got up very early in the morning to get out of the house before Daddy woke up. I took his dog for a long walk and we covered many miles of open green grass. She was a sweet natured dog, I gave her the affection that she needed and let her know that she was important to me. She was smiling and there was happiness in her eyes for a little while. I extended our walk because I did not want to go back to face Daddy, but there was no way to avoid it. On my return, I approached the house cautiously, knowing that he would be rehearsing his planned attack. I deliberately put the dog in the backyard and out of the way. It was better for her that she was not in the middle of the looming confrontation. I slowly entered the house, ready for him and sure enough, he was waiting for me.

Daddy was standing in the hall, electric blue eyes and twitching with his contained anger. The moment we came face to face he said: "Are you still fucking upset?". This was a provocation and I fell into his trap. I responded and said "You should be a better father". He exploded, screaming loudly and violently in my face with the purest rage. He said "Just fuck off out of here, get out of my house, you are all losers". His hate for me and his children was now being dramatically revealed. He wanted to hurt me, but he was a shrinking old man and I was not a child anymore. He moved to hit me but then he hesitated suddenly, realising that he could not dominate me physically.

I was ordered to leave, but as he attempted to escort me down the hall, I grabbed him by the throat with my right hand and pinned him to the wall. Now I was in control of our relationship and him, for the first time in my life. He was shocked and I could see that he was scrambling for a new strategy. He did not expect this from me. Whilst I had him pinned to the wall, I looked into his face and said, "So big man, are you going to throw me out of my own home?" He adjusted his behaviour instinctively, realising that he was at an unexpected disadvantage. With a lowered voice and altered body posture he submissively looked to the floor. He then said, "Well, I am just an old man with a bad heart, and I am asking you to leave". The chameleon switched characters in the blink of an eye.

Daddy then tried to wriggle out of my grip but I did not let him go. I told him that he was going to listen to me whether he liked it or not. I informed him that he was never a real father or deserving of love from his family. I then told him that Mammy would be turning in her grave if she could see his behaviour. This statement was intended to make him face his actions, but he spotted an opportunity. He said: "Well, your mother was no saint, she has plenty of skeletons in her closet”. This insult was so hideous and unbelievable, that I simply lost the power in my grip and my right arm fell down. His strategy worked and he quickly moved away and into the yard behind the house where he knew that he had space and potential weapons.

This attack on Mammy was so shocking that I could not speak for a few seconds. I just could not comprehend the poison that flowed from my father. I shouted at him “I will walk out of this house and I will not come back, you have just lost the one person who supported you”. He didn’t respond and I left immediately, never to return whilst he was alive. This was the second time that a conflict with my father made me leave home, but this time it was more serious. I finally found the courage to confront the tyrant and show him a side of me that he did not expect. Daddy knew that I could see him more clearly now, there was no hiding. Our relationship changed forever and there was no way back.

"Life Partner"

Despite my poor track record with women, a beautiful brown-eyed Polish girl came into my life in 2012, a year before my fight with Daddy. I was thirty-seven years old at that stage, she was six years younger and recently divorced following a terrible marriage. We met in work and a strong connection quickly formed. But I really tested her patience and commitment in the early stages. Addicts have a way of telling half-truths and glossing over important facts. We talked about going to clubs and I told her that I had used drugs in the past, but in a very general and vague way. I avoided detailing the scale of my cocaine use. Distractions and lies were used to mask my addiction in the first couple of years of our relationship.

It became harder to disguise my addiction after my partner moved in. I was sure that she was spotting the signs, phone switched off long periods, red raw skin around my nose and changing stories about where I had been. To avoid being caught in the act, I started to stay out all night, hanging around in seedy clubs, and giving all of my available cash to drug dealers and strippers. I also started isolating myself in hotel rooms for days, soaked to the bone in cocaine, alcohol and guilt. I was destroying our relationship because I did not believe that

I was worthy of a loving partner and the warmth of a safe home. But she stuck with me through all the drama, worried about me endlessly and screamed at me when I came home high and in a complete mess. I pushed her beyond what any person should have to deal with in a loving relationship, but she continued to believe in me and us.

"Counselling Therapy"

During the summer of 2015, I fell in the door on a Saturday morning after being missing in action for more than a day. I was unable to talk, blood running from my nose, wearing dirty clothes, stinking of alcohol and responsible for emptying my bank account. My partner was terrified and at the very edge of leaving me. After I sobered up, I agreed to start counselling therapy to try and save our relationship. Something different had to be done. This was an important step, but it came with disorientating consequences. We found a local therapist on the internet, a warm and gentle woman who gave me a good feeling from the first moment I sat down in front of her. I thought that I would need counselling therapy for a few weeks, a couple of months at the very most, but I remained in therapy solidly for two years.

Pain and guilt located in the past and deep in my subconsciousness were brought to the surface. I tried to resist the new reality that was opening up in front of me but there was nowhere to run. I am not ashamed to say that I cried a river of tears every week during and after each session. I avoided accepting any form of help over the years because I knew that facing the truth would shatter the ground beneath me and the lies that I clung to. As I opened up more and more, I relapsed badly and the cocaine binges got deeper. The compulsion seemed to come from nowhere. One minute, I was normal and then suddenly, I was in a bar, drinking aggressively and snorting cocaine off urine-stained toilet seats.

My therapist started to change direction. The questions became less about the death of Mammy and more about family dynamics and the role of my father. I was dismissive at first, but my therapist was now energised to go back to the start and explore everything. I remember we were having a conversation about Daddy, I was describing in a very matter-of-fact way how he got pleasure from humiliating Mammy and some of the lengths he went to deprive and abuse us. My therapist moved forward in her chair, this was a light bulb moment for her. She was trained to spot the traits of a dangerous personality disorder. When I provided more and more examples of his destructive nature, my therapist was visibly shocked. The tyranny of my father had been too overwhelming for me to understand and deal with as a child. I began to have many new feelings about my father, and myself. How could I not have seen who he really was? It was very unsettling to realise that I had been manipulated by a psychopath.

"Breakdown"

Despite living with addiction, I always worked hard. Being productive at work was something that replaced my lack of connection to family. A promotion eventually came my way, but I was not ready for the bigger responsibilities and the office politics I had to contend with. My anxiety went through the roof and the all or nothing drive took over. Getting up at 5 am to get to the office early, staying until 9 pm and working weekends from home was the new normal. I was determined to succeed at all costs. As my anxiety grew, my paranoia deepened and everything became tangled. I was over-trusting with the wrong colleagues, and this included using cocaine in their presence. Holding it all together was becoming impossible.

The increased stress impacted me physically, but I would not accept that I was struggling. I was suffering from unexplained body pain, inability to fight viruses, poor appetite and hardly sleeping. Terrible headaches visited me regularly and my neck was always unbearably cold. My colleagues would remark that I was constantly wearing a scarf in the office, which was strange considering that the office was kept at a normal room temperature. I have since learned that it was the increased stress hormone cortisol that was making my neck stiff and cold. My health was deteriorating rapidly and people were commenting that I had lost weight and looked exhausted.

The tide turned against me at work and I finally lost the strength to battle my way through. In desperation, I went to see a doctor and when I walked into his surgery, I immediately burst into tears before I could even take a chair. There was so much emotion being held down and inside, I was sobbing uncontrollably. After a few questions, the doctor signed me off without hesitation and I remained off work for several months. I just couldn't function and I retreated into myself. Fortunately, a director at work was sympathetic to my case and wanted to resolve the situation. It was agreed that I would leave with a generous settlement. I walked away from that job in the summer of 2016, feeling mostly relieved, but actually, much deeper problems were about to emerge. That settlement was more money in my bank account than I ever imagined was possible. An ideal opportunity to pay debts and make a fresh start, but an addict thinks very differently.

16. Going Back

This story began with my rock-bottom cocaine binge in the summer 2016. I locked myself in my London flat for six days and pushed my life to the edge, but I was saved. I now see that my drive for self-destruction was rooted in an instinct to avoid subconscious pain and the truth. There is a parallel story that makes me believe that my eternal mother had an even greater role in saving my life. A couple of weeks before my rock bottom binge in London, the Rebel went to see a psychic in Ireland for her own personal reasons. The psychic did not have any messages for my sister, instead, she shared a repeated warning from Mammy that I was in danger. There was no communication between the Rebel and myself over the years due to my relationship with Daddy. She did not know about the extent of my cocaine addiction at that stage. This message confused her and did not make any sense.

Whilst I was in the middle of my rock bottom binge in London, my partner was in Poland and unable to reach me by phone. She contacted the Rebel to ask for help in desperation. The cocaine problem was now out in the open and the warning from Mammy suddenly made sense. When I finally came out of the binge and switched my phone on, there was several messages from the Rebel asking me to call her. I could hear the upset and desperation in her voice when we eventually spoke. She then proceeded to tell me about the warning she received from Mammy through the psychic. I was stunned and intrigued by this information, and something told me that I must go back to Ireland to see the Rebel as soon as possible.

A few days later, I drove to North Wales to take the ferry and landed in Dublin. I stayed with the Rebel, which was a little uncomfortable initially, as we had never spent any time together in the past. But my curiosity drove me forward and I wanted to know about the message she received from the psychic. Once we started talking, so much came out. We both shared a desire to understand each other better and clarify secrets and mysteries within the family. The Rebel had many boxes of old photographs which helped to trigger conversations and go down some dark roads. Being ten years older than me, she had such a different perspective on the overall family. I learned that the rest of the family knew much more than me and they did not trust me with sensitive information because I was so loyal to my father.

Daddy was the main subject in our conversations whilst I stayed with her for a couple of days. I had to acknowledge that I had a very narrow view of the family and that I wilfully denied my father's tyranny for most of my life. We also talked about Mammy and the hardship that my father inflicted on her. This was difficult to discuss because I felt guilty that I did not challenge my father. I blindly supported an obvious tyrant. But the Rebel reminded me that I was a child when Daddy shaped me for his own selfish needs. This was very upsetting and many new memories of my childhood started to come to the surface. These painful episodes were buried deeply to avoid contending with them. But this strategy doesn't work in the long term. Storing up these negative feelings leaves no space for good to enter my life.

"Unexpected Author"

I told the Rebel that I had recently developed a strong urge to write, which was a huge surprise to her, and me. This was not the identity I had established. I started with some awkward and emotional poetry, but I never dared to believe that I could become an author. Writing and the world of books was completely foreign to me. After my school and college years finished, I never picked up a book or developed myself. Writing helped me to go back through the chaos of my life and confront the reality of my childhood. This was the start of a difficult process to cut my father out of my existence and consign him to history. When you let go of your parents, regardless of their character or influence on your life, the result is that you are now on your own in the world. I felt like I had just woken up from a nightmare and it was a sobering crash back down to earth. A determination to make a positive change began to burn inside of me.

I started writing this story with some purpose in late 2016. The first few months were dedicated to capturing the most salient childhood memories, in no particular order. Once I had some basic work completed, I then developed each episode into a structure of chronological chapters. At night, more and more memories came to me through my dreams and then crystallised into conscious thoughts when I woke up in the morning. Sometimes I would wake up at 5 am, bursting with new content and commence writing on my laptop all day. There was so much to write and process, I could not stop. The trauma was being pulled up and out of my stomach, into my chest and then pushed out of my body through my arms and hands. As I found the words to express everything, it was like removing poison from my body.

The first draft was completed about one year later. Once I got going, everything just poured out of me and onto the page. The profound experiences that I went through were constantly amazing to me, even though it was a story about my own life. I could hardly believe it was me who endured such trauma as a child and acted in such a destructive way as an adult. When I printed the raw manuscript for the first time, I sat down, stared at it and cried. I had transferred a lifetime of confusion and pain into the orderly pages bound together in front of me. The first draft was tangled and very long. The story needed lots of reading and edits. I re-visited every sentence, paragraph and chapter multiple times to investigate the emotions and motivations in my writing.

The entire process was very cathartic, and the story became my new best friend for the next few years. I looked forward to diving in at every opportunity and it really helped me to identify all the problems that created such a chaotic adult. The sequence of events that always led me to using cocaine in the past became more detectable. The process of editing was also very helpful.

As the quality of the book improved, my life improved, it became part of me. Previously, the thought of focusing on a book made me anxious. But things changed for the better and I read many books about psychology and addiction to understand the forces that controlled me. It pointed to psychological injuries that caused survival adaptations. My ego and automated resistance strategy were coping mechanisms to avoid painful memories. Once I had identified this problem, it was possible to understand how I could change and heal properly. With better self-awareness, I observed any addictive motivations as they arose and headed them off to keep my recovery on track.

I got back to work and I managed to achieve a more balanced approach to my professional life. The old "all or nothing" mantra and fight or flight tendencies were mostly kept at bay. This allowed me to enjoy work on a day-to-day basis and avoid the politics and conflicts that used to draw me in so easily. Working and being able to pay my bills was a crucial part of my recovery. Borrowing, using credit cards and wild spending was simply not an option for me moving forward. I had to learn how to see money as a practical tool and not as an emotional opportunity to obtain a quick buzz. When my wages hit my account every month, I gave my partner most of my earnings to disrupt previously ingrained behaviour. This cut the head off the snake before it became an all-consuming monster.

My partner and I moved to South London in 2018. We got a rescue dog, a beautiful female German

Shepherd cross who came all the way from Poland. I have to say, her arrival and my relationship with her have supported my recovery more than I can understand. It gave me responsibility and a connection to nature that had been missing from my life for decades. The addiction and compulsions that previously controlled me faded. Alcohol, cocaine and spending money were replaced with more natural stimulants. I slowly taught myself how to rewire my head and activate dopamine in new ways. Visits to a beach or a walk in the forest with my partner and our dog became my new version of joy.

As my recovery started to look more and more stable from 2019 onwards, my partner and I decided to try for a baby. This was a very natural step for my partner, a warm and loving person from a functional family. I always formed playful relationships with kids, but having a child was a responsibility that I avoided. At the back of my mind, I could still remember a conversation I had with my father during a visit to Ireland a few years after Mammy died. We were chatting in the kitchen late at night, he was slagging off my siblings and his grandchildren and I was trying to stay neutral. I diverted the conversation by saying that I would like to have my own children in the future. Daddy looked at me with a certain vicious delight, there was a sparkle in his eyes. He then crushed me with "You love yourself too much to have children", looked away and laughed to himself. I did not respond to him at that time, but he really cut me down.

We were delighted to discover that my partner had become pregnant as we approached Christmas 2020. It was such an amazing feeling, we found ourselves constantly staring at each other with a sense of wonder. The anticipation of such a beautiful arrival immediately became the centre of our world. However, tragically, we lost that pregnancy at just seven weeks. It was an ectopic pregnancy and my partner had to endure surgery. We were completely devastated and it would now become more challenging to conceive. Time was not on our side and part of me felt that I did not deserve the gift of a child and fatherhood. What my father had said to me kept coming into my mind and haunting my thoughts.

17. New Life

Following the pain and the loss of the ectopic pregnancy, my partner and I supported each other and we pushed forward together. I successfully left the terror of relapses further and further in the past and life settled into a place of stability. Everything was fine on the surface, but there was some unfinished business for me. Daddy was still alive and his dark shadow loomed as strong as ever. I was told that his physical health was deteriorating, but I did not entertain any thoughts of making contact, that would be a lie. He needed more help as the years progressed, but his aggressive nature only seemed to harden with age. The Rebel told me that my name came up in conversation and my father remarked that I had not been in contact for many years. He looked away dismissively and said, “Patrick could be dead or in jail”. I am sure that these were two of the possible outcomes that he wanted for me.

The Robot and the Rattlesnake pretended to take care of my father from a safe distance after Mammy died. They crept and conspired to gain favour and line themselves up to benefit from his assets when he passed. Daddy could see them coming from a mile away, their greedy enthusiasm amused him. They spent ten years sending him cooked meals and sucking up, but he cut them off as soon as he had a better option. Surprisingly, the Rebel became the one that my father leaned on most towards the end of his life. He demanded her attention and she had to be on call at all times, with support from her husband. The Rebel had the opportunity to punish her father for the neglect, humiliation and violent abuse, but she didn't allow that history to define her. She played the game and she did not let him pull her down into his world of resentment and misery.

Daddy was selective about the help that he required, he only wanted the Rebel to do the things that he couldn't, and nothing more than that. He continued to live alone and our family home deteriorated to a state that matched his inner world, cold, filthy, hostile and strange. If anyone offered to help they were accused of wanting something and being a "circling vulture". Daddy's mind stayed lucid and sharp, but his paranoia deepened towards the end. He implemented an elaborate and deliberately complicated locking system. The outside gate leading to the road was secured with a padlock and chain as a first level of defence. Then there were a further ten separate keys to access the front door and every internal door in the house. Each room was locked at all times, just like a jail. His final action before he went to sleep at night was to deploy a crude sliding iron bar across his bedroom door to barricade himself inside.

"The Call"

I was driving in central London on Sunday 8th May 2022 when I received a call from the Rebel to report that Daddy had been rushed to hospital with severe stomach pains. His bowels had ruptured and his organs were failing, he was near the end. It was such a sudden and strange feeling, I had very mixed emotions. The boy in me was upset and nervous, and wanted to travel to Ireland to see him and reconcile. But the man that I had developed through recovery was more rational, and accepted that my journey would be wasted on someone who did not feel love towards his own children. A voice inside me told me that it was better for everyone that he slipped away quickly. I had already grieved for the loss of a fairy tale father.

The Rebel was the only sibling that stayed with him in the hospital. Despite their relationship, she wanted to be there at the end. This was her chance to finally get the upper hand and be in control of him. I don't judge my siblings who stayed away, he abused all of us and everyone reacted to the news differently. A few of his grandchildren visited him through the night to say goodbye. They knew that he was a strange man, and maybe they were aware of his destructive behaviour, but they were outside of the direct damage we endured. I was told that he was visibly scared at the end, death was coming and he knew it. He was breathing violently and fighting for his life.

I hardly slept that night, I was occupied by a weird energy. Part of me felt relief and wanted him to be dead, but there was also a very hollow and subdued feeling. When I woke up at 6 am on Monday, I knew that he was dead, the tension I felt the night before had somehow lifted. A few minutes later, the Rebel called and confirmed that my instinct was correct. My father, a man of ninety-one years, was gone from this world. When

Mammy died fifteen years before, I went to Ireland alone and acted as Daddy's enforcer and family referee at the funeral. This role stopped me from dealing with my own emotions and grief. However, on this occasion, my partner travelled to Ireland with me, which made things feel very different. We landed in Dublin early Tuesday morning following the car journey and ferry overnight. My first stop was to visit Mammy's grave and ask her for the strength to face the next few days.

Daddy left strict instructions that he wanted to be cremated with no religious service. He knew that he was not widely loved or respected, his shallow public veneer had dissolved after Mammy died. Despite his instructions, in typical Rebel style, my sister organised some traditional funeral rituals. His body was held in an open coffin in the funeral parlour for a few hours for anyone who wanted to see him. The last time I saw my father was nine years before, and I had my right hand around his throat, pinning him to the wall. But I knew that I had to face him for one last time. My partner and I drove to the funeral parlour, parked outside and I took a deep breath to prepare myself before going in.

I was ushered into a large room by a nice woman who worked there. It was a dark and silent room, with candles placed around the edge to create a solemn atmosphere. The open coffin with my father's body was positioned in the middle of the room like an island. It was just me and him there together, like old times. His body was packed neatly into the wooden box, eyes shut with a cement and indignant expression on his face. He had been cleaned up nicely, shirt and tie, a haircut, shaved, and his skin was somehow amazingly smooth and clear. Seeing him again after so many years made me nervous initially. I walked around the coffin cautiously, circling the enemy to make sure that he was unable to attack. I then stood over the coffin and built up the courage to touch the tyrant. My first move was to place my right hand on his chest, I wanted to test that he was truly dead. I gave him a push, but there was no response. I then progressed and clasped his cold fleshy face in my right hand. My touch was not gentle or with love, it was firm and designed to send a clear message. You are not in control now.

The cremation was held the next day. It was a partial family gathering of his children and grandchildren. As expected, some of my siblings continued to stay away.

There were two old colleagues from his days in the military who I didn't recognise and an officer also present. The officer attendance was not from a place of respect, officer funeral attendance was compulsory for every retired soldier. The Robot made an appearance, but he kept it very low-key, avoiding eye contact and conversation with me. The Rattlesnake did not show her nasty face. I was partly surprised that she missed the opportunity to say goodbye to her lover, the tyrant that she admired so much when he was in his prime. Perhaps she sensed that I would have ordered her to leave and she avoided a public humiliation.

Daddy's death brought many old memories to the surface for me. Memories that I had filed away as insignificant at the time, but suddenly had new context and meaning. I remembered being in the car with him as a teenager as he drove past the Robot out jogging on a Saturday afternoon. Daddy looked at his son with a combination of distaste and personal satisfaction. He ridiculed the Robot in front of me, laughing at his existence and attempt to be fit and healthy. He said "look at that fool out jogging, what is he running away from?". He said this knowing that his son was running away from the monstrous reality that his father had possessed his wife for his own dark pleasure and amusement.

The service was short, with some readings from a couple of grandchildren and some very inappropriate music. Someone told them to play Time to Say Goodbye by Andrea Bocelli and Sarah Brightman. It was hard not to laugh whilst the song seemed to go on forever. Daddy hated music. It was then up to me to say the final words before his body would be sent through the curtain and committed to the flames. This specific responsibility was not something that I had planned for, but the Rebel asked me to do it. I prepared some words that morning, not wanting to be angry in an obvious way, but I made sure that I spoke the truth. This is what I said.

“Daddy was the product of a fierce mother and brutal father. A man of two sides, powerful and capable in public, but his inner world was complicated and divisive. He made his children pick sides and he carried his own childhood suffering into his adult life. Mammy was the contrast to his world, loyal, loving, and forgiving. They were two actors in a pantomime that we all lived through. But her love was not enough, even at ninety-one, he never softened. Pay attention, there is meaning in death. Daddy had a deep and profound role in the lives of his children, and his grandchildren, as a consequence. We ask ourselves, what parts of Daddy will we miss, and what parts do we need to let go of".

As I spoke, I looked at the faces gathered there. Some people looked confused and some had open mouths in shock. The Rebel looked visibly delighted that the truth was finally being spoken in public. I stared at the Robot, he closed his eyes and looked at the floor, hoping that I would not go too far and point to Daddy's relationship with his wife. He was relieved when I walked away from the microphone. The mixed reactions to my speech summed up the dysfunction in my family and how my father manipulated his public image. After the service was over there was no family gathering to celebrate his life or share old stories about a great man. Inside we all felt the same, we were thankful that he left us so suddenly.

My father's house needed to be straightened out after his death. I joined some of my siblings there to get on with an unpleasant task. It was so strange, we felt like intruders in the place that used to be our home. It felt so cold, my skin was crawling, and it was hard to contemplate that I grew up there. Daddy was a filthy man and a dedicated hoarder. The garden was wild and overgrown and his sheds were packed to the roof with broken furniture and hazardous rubbish. The kitchen was stocked with rotten food and mystery liquids in rusty metal tins. Every available cupboard and drawer contained soiled and musty clothes. An industrial level clean-up was required.

Multiple large skips were ordered and we managed to clear out everything. When the work was done, all that remained was the ghostly shell of a loveless home in disrepair. Nobody wanted to live there now, that was out of the question. It was obvious that it would be sold and hopefully, the new owner would invest, knock it down and remove the rotten parts. I was sure that I would drive by in the future and see something better constructed in that miserable space.

My father died a wealthy man, a lifetime of greed and consistently depriving his family built up a surprisingly large estate for a working-class man. We found complex diary notes and strange drawings detailing the movement of cash from his multiple accounts. He spent his evenings analysing his assets and double checking the numbers. Not surprisingly, we found absolutely nothing in the house that could be categorised as sentimental. This was the cold evidence that his money was all that existed in his mind. His death and departure happened so fast, but better that way. Business had been taken care of.

About two months after my father died, I was walking through London in between work meetings, when I received a very special text message. My partner informed me that she was expecting with a photo of a positive pregnancy test. I called immediately and I could feel the smile beaming on her face as we talked excitedly about the joy that was about to fill our world. The pregnancy was tense at times after the ectopic pregnancy before, we were so careful and focused. It brought us closer together and provided undeniable motivation to take my continued recovery even more seriously.

"Happy Birthday"

Our daughter Aurelia arrived on the 12th of March 2023, my mother's birthday, a gift of pure gold. If I was looking for a sign that Mammy was still watching over me, this would be a sweet reminder every year. As a mark of respect, Aurelia was christened in Ireland and in the same church that hosted Mummy's funeral. The christening was on Sunday 18th February, the same day and date Mammy died seventeen years before. We asked the Rebel to be godmother and she gladly accepted. It was a beautiful and magical day. At the end of the christening, I walked around the church with my daughter in my arms, holding her tightly and standing in the places where Mammy used to be. I am not religious in the traditional or Catholic sense, but I could feel Mammy with us. Aurelia was so quiet, but very alert and interested in everything, almost like she was aware of something powerful around her.

Witnessing my childhood and confronting the objective facts through writing has helped me to understand that Daddy was a strange and heartless man. When my partner told me that she was pregnant, my immediate role was to protect and provide for mother and baby. This was automatic and a force of nature that is greater than my own will. It is completely alien to me to contemplate manipulating or abusing my partner and our child to serve my selfish needs. But that is exactly what my father did with all my family throughout his life. I can now see that I subconsciously resisted love and becoming a father because of the experience I went through as a child and my relationship with him.

When Mammy died, it took so many years to deal with the grief. The pain of that loss crippled me for such a long time. When Daddy died, his hollow spirit just evaporated and it felt very final. It's hard to describe, but I immediately felt unburdened, stripped back and lighter. Even my relationship with Ireland improved when he departed. My native land was a place that used to represent painful memories and a place to avoid.

Suddenly the beauty and importance of Ireland became much more apparent to me.

History repeats itself and behaviour is automatically passed on through generations. Boys are shaped by the role of their father and negative patterns from the past continue, if they are not acknowledged and confronted. I accept that my father and his father were bad men and they are both part of my DNA. I am a direct descendant, but at my core, I know that I am capable of being a good man. I am not a victim and I will not allow my father's shadow to define me as I move forward. Telling the truth in this story has saved me from addiction and allowed me to become the man I must be.

Acknowledgements

My partner, Agnieszka, must be given the highest acknowledgement. She pushed me to accept help and weathered the storm of many relapses. Without her love and patience, I would not have found a way through. I would like to thank my counselling therapist, Lou Campbell MBACP. Her authentic approach, warmth and expertise helped me to understand how my emotional behaviour developed. Our Saturday morning sessions were full of tears, laughs and revelations. I learned so much talking with her and I am forever grateful.

The Rebel clarified many facts that have distorted our historical sense of family. Her contribution helped me to untangle my childhood memories. It was very surprising and unlikely that we have come together to face our family dysfunction, but I am glad that it happened. Several friends have seen me at my lowest point and they have helped me through the most difficult years. Some have read the early raw and tangled manuscript and encouraged me to become an author. Cecilia Istria-Dorland must be given special thanks. A dark story shared whilst walking our dogs on the weekend has become a transformative creative project with her support.

Annie O'Sullivan

1931 - 2007

I dedicate this story to Mammy. A warm and resilient woman who loved and nourished all of her children. She endured my father's lifelong abuse and a devastating family betrayal which would have destroyed many women. But in the end, she was stronger and her spirit prevailed.

Printed in Great Britain
by Amazon

46358623R00225